N

MW00777434

No Fair City

Dark Stories from Perth's Past

Gary Knight

TIPPERMUIR
· BOOKS LIMITED ·

This first edition published and copyright 2017 by
Tippermuir Books Ltd, Perth, Scotland.
mail@tippermuirbooks.co.uk
www.tippermuirbooks.co.uk

Editorial and Project Management: Dr Paul S. Philippou.
Project Support: Ajay Close, Jean Hands, and Steve Zajda.
Illustrations: Lynne Knight.
Photography: Roben Antoniewicz.
Cover design: Matthew Mackie.

ISBN: 978-0-9954623-5-9 (paperback)
A CIP catalogue record for this book is available
from the British Library.

Text styling and artwork by
Bernard Chandler [graffik], Glastonbury, England.
Text set in Photina 9.5pt on 14pt.
Printed in Great Britain by CPI Group (UK) Ltd, Croydon CR0 4YY

DEDICATION

FOR MY SONS
JACOB AND FINNAN

ACKNOWLEDGEMENTS

First of all, I would like to thank all the staff
of Perth & Kinross Council Archive and the
Local & Family History section of the AK Bell Library
who are always very accommodating and helpful.

Next, I would like to thank all at Tippermuir Books,
especially Paul Philippou for taking a chance
with me on my first book.

Enormous thanks goes to my wife Lynne for
drawing the illustrations, checking my grammar
and spelling before sending it to the publishers,
and for all her support and encouragement.

I would also like to thank George Penny and
Robert Scott Fittis whose excellent books on
Perth and Perthshire inspired me to write my own.

Lastly, to the victims of dreadful injustice,
accident and crime in Perth who all
deserve to be remembered.

CONTENTS

CHAPTER ONE

Kings Under Attack

A CASTLE LOST

The city of Perth owes its existence to its location being the first point where the mighty River Tay could be bridged downstream.

TO PROTECT this important crossing, a castle was built, a royal castle no less. The city developed around the castle, as merchants and tradesmen moved in to supply its occupants with goods. The city flourished, ships navigated along the river importing and exporting goods to and from Perth.

Perth was at the mercy of the river as flooding has been a major problem until very recently. One savage flood swept down river in the year 1210 and hit the city with such force that the castle was washed away completely. King William I (the Lion) was in residence at the time. Fourteen members of his household were drowned and tragically his youngest son was lost to the dark, ice-cold waters. The king only escaped with his eldest son by clambering onto a boat. Flooding in Perth was a constant threat so the castle was never properly rebuilt and used to its full potential.

Flooding continued to hit Perth until £25 million was spent on flood defences after a huge flood devastated the city in 1993. Let us hope flooding in Perth is now a thing of the past. If you look at the Old Bridge (also known as Perth Bridge or Smeaton's Bridge) by the North Inch, carved on the stonework are the high-water levels from past floods.

Opposite: Huntingtower Castle.

THE BLACK PARLIAMENT

King Robert the Bruce had all the nobility in Scotland put their seals to the Declaration of Arbroath in 1320.

THIS ACT was to show the Pope that Scotland was united in its stance against English claims of overlordship. Behind the scenes, the Scots were anything but unified. To gain the throne, Bruce had in 1306 murdered his political rival John Comyn at the High Altar of the Greyfriars Kirk in Dumfries. This sparked a civil war in Scotland between the Bruce and Comyn factions. The Comyns were the most powerful family in the land and loyal to the disposed but rightful king of Scotland, John Balliol, who in 1296 had been forced to give up his crown by Edward I of England. When Bruce passed a law that no member of the Scottish nobility could own land in both Scotland and England, many Scottish nobles lost land. These lords became known as the Disinherited.

Although by 1320 Robert the Bruce was winning his war with England, there was still the potential for resistance to his regime. When the Earl of Dunbar was in France meeting the Pope, he heard of a plot back in Scotland to overthrow Robert the Bruce by the disinherited lords. Arrests were made, including Agnes Comyn, the Countess of Strathearn, who turned King's evidence and named the other plotters. The conspirators were rounded up and taken to Scone where they were tried in what was to become known as the Black Parliament. They were forced to confess and then sentenced.

Sir William Soulis and his aunt were imprisoned for life. Sir Roger Mowbray, who, although by his trial had died of natural causes, was taken to Scone on a litter. He was tried, found guilty of treason, and his corpse hanged, drawn, and quartered. Sir David Brechin, Sir Gilbert Malherbe, and Sir John Logie were all tied to the tails of horses and dragged through the streets of Perth before being taken up to the Burghmuir (then known as the Bourghmuir) where they were hanged and beheaded. Vast crowds from Perth made their way to the high ground to the west of the city to see some of the most important people in the land executed.

Motte and bailey castle with River Tay flowing past.

Robert the Bruce was swift and ruthless. He showed little mercy to the conspirators. The Countess of Strathearn, although allowed to live, was cast in irons and thrown into the dungeon of Strathearn Castle to end her days in a damp, cold cell. The site of this castle stood between the town of Crieff and village of Comrie. Now a tall, needle-like monument to Sir David Baird, a late eighteenth/early nineteenth century British military commander, sits on top of the hill, and no remnants of the castle survive. However, it was reported that when they were erecting the memorial to Baird, workmen broke into a lost vault and found human remains and relics, belonging perhaps to the unfortunate Countess of Strathearn.

A MURDEROUS KING?

Several of the many histories of Perth written in the Victorian era narrate the story of a murder at the High Altar of St John's Kirk.

THE VICTIM was the Earl of Cornwall and he was alleged to have been killed by his brother, King Edward III of England. The reason was said to have been Cornwall's burning down of Lesmahagow Abbey, which was full of Scottish refugees seeking sanctuary during the Second War of Scottish Independence. This war crime enraged the English king who during an argument stabbed the earl to death.

It is a good story but unfortunately seems to be a piece of Wars of Scottish Independence propaganda. Edward of England was said to be heartbroken by his brother's death and it is now thought that although the Earl of Cornwall did die whilst in Perth (in 1337), it was as the result of catching a fever.

REGICIDE

By far the worst crime committed within what is now the city of Perth was the assassination of James I of Scotland in the winter of 1437.

THE CRIME OF REGICIDE, the killing of a monarch, was almost unheard of in Scotland. People were horrified by the actions of the main conspirator against the king, the Earl of Atholl. To them, his treason was so incomprehensible that they had to justify it and in a superstitious age the only reason for his crime would be if somehow Atholl were bewitched. So, a supernatural element came into the story.

It is interesting to note that whenever a great disaster hits Scotland, stories of warnings from the other world often surface. Alexander III, whose death without an adult heir in 1286 led to decades of war with

England, was said to have been warned not to travel one stormy night by an old hag. He did not heed the warning, wet rocks caused his horse to slip on a cliff path and King Alexander was thrown to his death. At Alexander's wedding in Jedburgh Castle, the story goes that the Grim Reaper himself showed up and warned the king of his impending doom. There are later examples too. Before an unknown assassin murdered James III of Scotland after his defeat at the Battle of Sauchieburn in 1488, a witch had warned him that he would soon die. Many years later when his son, James IV of Scotland, led his army on the disastrous invasion of England and ultimate defeat at the Battle of Flodden (1513), the Devil himself was said to have appeared on Edinburgh's market cross and warned the nation of approaching doom.

It is not unusual for a paranormal element to be weaved into the fabric of these stories but the truth is James I was deeply unpopular. His father, Robert III, despite being the grandson of Robert the Bruce, was a weak king who lost power to his brother, the Duke of Albany, James's uncle. Albany had the king's eldest son, James's big brother, David the Duke of Rothesay, murdered in Falkland Castle. For his safety, James, then a young boy, was sent to France. En route, he was captured by English pirates and handed over to Henry IV of England. The English kept James a prisoner for eighteen years. This allowed Albany to gain complete control of the realm when Robert III died. The Duke of Albany did nothing to secure the release of his nephew, so after Albany's death, James was finally set free and was crowned at Scone in 1424. The king turned on his kinsmen, the Albany Stewarts. Some were executed, while others fled. James I set very high taxes to pay a ransom to the English and, perhaps not wanting to be like his weak father, was harsh, ruthless, and made many enemies.

The tale goes that on one dark and cold winter's night, Walter Stewart, the Earl of Atholl, was riding to his lands north of Perth. He saw what looked like the twinkling of the flames from a fire in the distance and thought it would be good to stop and get a wee heat around that fire. He hoped he might be offered something to eat and perhaps a warm drink but as he arrived at the campfire, he was surprised to see, sat around the fire, three witches.

'Ah Atholl! What took you so long?', cackled one.

'Yes, we have been waiting a long time for you!' , hissed another.

The third simply stirred a pot that was bubbling over the fire. Atholl was terrified but somehow the witches persuaded him to dismount and sit by the fire, for they had a tale for his ears only. The three witches told the Earl of Atholl that someday he would be king of Scotland, for they could see him wearing a crown. This was incredible, for although Atholl was related to the king, he was not the next in line to the throne. In fact, it was very unlikely that Atholl would ever be king. He went home to his castle but could not get the witches' story out of his mind.

'Perhaps they were right and it is my destiny to become king', he thought.

Convincing himself that one day he might indeed wear the crown, he made plans to kill the king when he next came to Perth.

In February of 1437, despite being warned by an Irish witch not to journey north, James I came to Perth to hold a parliament. As there was no comfortable castle where the king could reside whilst in Perth, he stayed in the Blackfriary situated just outside the safety of the city walls.

On the night of 20 February 1437, the king was in the queen's bedchambers – the royals were talking together and being fussed over by the ladies-in-waiting. The royal couple were deep in conversation, unaware that dark shadows were making their way across planks of wood, which had been laid across the moat that protected the friary. Men silently climbed over the wall, then ran across the courtyard. When they came to the main door, they found it unlocked – this was part of the plan. The king's chamberlain, whose job it was to protect the king, was in on Atholl's murderous scheme. The double-crossing chamberlain had laid the planks across the moat.

The first thing that alerted the king was the sound of his guards being overpowered in the corridor outside the royal apartments. James sprang from his chair by the fire, ran to open the door, and saw his guards lying on the floor of the corridor, dead or dying, and armed men running towards the royal chambers. Quickly he slammed shut the door and looked for the bar that went across the door, resting in two slots thus locking it. But, the bar was gone – again the chamberlain's work. With no means to secure the door, James panicked. He did not know what to do, then one of the queen's ladies-in-waiting, a girl named Katherine Douglas,* ran up to the door. She put her slender white arm in the two sockets for the bar.

Outside the room, the would-be assassins pushed the door but something stopped it. They ran at the door and it flew open. Katherine Douglas's arm broke with a loud snap, her arm dangled limply at her side as the armed men rushed into the room. They roughly pushed the protesting queen aside and hunted for the king but they could not find him. He seemed to have escaped. They turned the room upside down, smashing furniture and ripping off wall hangings from the walls – but to no avail. Then one man pulled up a rug on the floor and underneath a trapdoor was discovered. They opened the trapdoor and went down the stairs into the cellars and sewers. There they found the king hiding. He fought bravely but was stabbed sixteen times by the assassins, who seeing the king die, fled the scene.

The biggest mistake the regicides made was leaving the queen alive, as she and her supporters subsequently arrested everyone involved in the killing. The Earl of Atholl was taken to Edinburgh and found guilty of high treason. His sentence was to be put to death over three days.

---

* *Katherine Douglas was then known locally as Kate Bar-lass.*

EXECUTION OF THE EARL OF ATHOLL

On the morning of 26 March 1437, the Earl of Atholl was taken from his cell in Edinburgh Castle to the city's market cross.

AT THE CROSS stood a big wooden crane, from its arm a rope dangled down to head height. The Edinburgh hangman or Doomster as he was known in the capital, tied the rope to Atholl's legs. The Doomster hoisted the earl high up into the air before letting go of the rope. Atholl plummeted towards the ground, stopping with his head a few inches from the hard earth. This was done repeatedly. The strain on Atholl's body caused most of his bones to be ripped from their sockets. In agony, he was cut down and taken back to his cell. He must have lain on the hard, cold, cell floor that night in abject misery and unimaginable pain.

His ordeal had only begun, for the next day he was dragged down to the market cross on a hurdle (a type of sledge).

At the cross, was a fire basket and on the white-hot coals sat a red-hot iron crown. Atholl was held roughly, as the Doomster, using a pair of pliers, lifted the crown and placed it on Atholl's head. The taste of burning flesh would have stuck in the back of onlookers' throats and the smell of cooking meat would have been gut wrenching. The screams from Atholl's twisted and contorted mouth echoed up and down the Royal Mile. After the crown cooled, it was pulled from the earl's head.

When the crown was removed, branded on the Earl of Atholl's head were the words:

'King of Traitors'.

It seems the witches were right after all – Atholl did get to wear the crown. Some accounts go on to tell of Atholl being blinded before he was taken back to his cell. He probably looked forward to the release that death would bring him the next day. On the third day, Atholl was taken one last time to the Cross of Edinburgh, where he was hanged until almost dead, cut down, and placed on a table. The Doomster cut off Atholl's clothes and, with a small hooked knife, castrated him. Next, the Doomster stabbed the unfortunate earl below the navel and ran his knife up the earl's body. The wound was pulled apart and Atholl was disembowelled. The Earl of Atholl, who was still alive, probably smelt his own entrails as they burned in the fire beside him. As he lay dying on the table, Atholl's still beating heart was ripped out and burned. The now very much dead earl was beheaded and his head placed on a spike on top of Edinburgh's main city gate. Atholl's body was cut into four pieces, one quarter was placed on another gate in the Scottish capital, the others were sent to Perth, Stirling, and Aberdeen to garnish the entrance to those cities and act as a grim warning.

* * *

EXECUTION OF SIR ROBERT GRAHAM

Sir Robert Graham was the chief assassin and when he was caught he fared little better than the Earl of Atholl.

HE WAS TAKEN to Stirling, chained to the market cross, whereupon the city's hangman pulled out all of his teeth with a pair of pliers. Graham then had red-hot iron pins driven into his body; big red bubbles of blood formed in his toothless mouth as he screamed in agony. When

this was done, Graham had his flesh ripped open, likely with a tool known as the Cats Claw. Not wanting Graham to die or pass out from loss of blood, the executioner ran a red-hot knife over Graham's torn flesh to clot and stem the flow of blood. Finally, Graham had his hand nailed to the back of a cart and was dragged up to the Gowan Hill to be decapitated on the beheading stone, which is still there to this day. His lifeless body, like Atholl's,

was cut into quarters and publicly displayed throughout Scotland.

The torture and executions of those involved in the murder of James I were unusually brutal and savage, even for those times. But the public had to see these men suffer horrifically, as their punishments sent out a clear warning from the Crown as to what could be expected it you took the life of Scotland's monarch. James's son, also named James, was crowned James II of Scotland, not at the usual spot at Scone but at Holyrood Abbey in Edinburgh, well away from the Perthshire lands of Atholl.

James I was buried in Perth. He was laid to rest within the grounds of the Carthusian Monastery he founded in 1429. His queen, Joan Beaufort, was also interned there, as was Margaret Tudor the queen of James IV of Scotland. A monument memorialising these burials stands by the

King James IV Hospital, which sits on the original site of the monastery.

A plaque detailing the murder of James I is situated on a wall, which overlooks the North Inch, at the bottom of Blackfriars Street where it meets Charlotte Street. The plaque also commemorates another gruesome event in Perth's history, the Battle of the Clans, which will feature in the next chapter.

THE RUTHVEN RAID

In August of 1582, the 16-year-old James VI
(future James I of England) was hunting in Atholl.

THE EARL OF GOWRIE turned up and offered the young king hospitality at Ruthven Castle, which sits to the west of Perth and is today known as Huntingtower Castle. The king accepted the offer and rode with the earl to the castle. When the king was safely within the stronghold of Ruthven, he was seized by Gowrie and locked up. This was a coup by a group of Protestant lords, who wanted to control the king due to their belief that the king was surrounding himself with men who might not be openly Catholic but had Catholic leanings, chiefly the king's cousin, and perhaps lover, a Frenchman named Esme Stuart, who the king had made the Duke of Lennox.

Amongst the conspirators were the powerful Earl of Mar, the Master of Glamis, Lord Boyd, and Lord Lindsay. They styled themselves the Lords Enterprisers and had support from the Scottish Kirk and even the queen of England, Elizabeth I. James, who was reduced to tears, was rebuked by being told it was better *'bairns greet than bearded men'*. The Lords Enterprises made the king sign a declaration stating he was not being held against his will, although he clearly was. James was also forced to order the Duke of Lennox to leave Scotland. The exiled duke died in Paris a year later and his embalmed heart was sent to the king who was devastated by the death of his friend. The Lords Enterprisers held the king captive for ten months, though not solely at Ruthven Castle: as time rolled by, the king found himself being held in more comfortable surroundings; he was held at Gowrie House where the Sheriff Court now stands in Tay Street and Falkland Palace.

Allowing the king more comfort was the undoing of his captors. When he was at Falkland Palace, the king was permitted to go to a feast at St Andrews. He had secretly informed some of his supporters of his intended visit. When he arrived at St Andrews, he made his way to the castle, which was held by his followers. Once there he was safe. The Lords Enterprisers now threw themselves on the king's mercy, which was surprisingly granted. The Lords Enterprisers continued to plot against the king and were involved in a plan to capture Stirling Castle. The king marched against them with an army and the Lords were forced into exile. The Earl of Gowrie was not so lucky: he was taken to Edinburgh and executed for treason. After this, you might have thought that the Ruthvens would have kept a low profile regarding James VI but not so as the next story demonstrates.

THE GOWRIE CONSPIRACY

The Gowrie Conspiracy is one of the strangest events involving a monarch in Perth. It seems to have been an attempt on the life of James VI but perhaps all is not as it seems.

ON THE MORNING of 5 August 1600, James VI was setting off from Falkland Palace with some friends to enjoy a day's hunting when a lone horseman approached. This rider turned out to be the Master of Ruthven. Ruthven dismounted and proceeded to tell the king a strange story. This tale was about a black man who had been apprehended in a field outside Perth. This man had been trying to bury a pitcher full of gold coins. The man was taken to Gowrie House, which was a large turreted town house owned by the Master of Ruthven's brother, the Earl of Gowrie. The king was intrigued and agreed to come to Perth and interrogate the stranger.

The royal party set off for Perth. When they arrived at Gowrie House, they were met by the Earl of Gowrie who invited them all for lunch. As they sat around the table eating, the conversation must have been dominated by talk of the prisoner locked up in one of the turreted rooms on the top floor. After they had dined, the Master of Ruthven and the king went upstairs to speak to the mysterious man, while Gowrie and the king's party went into the orchard.

As the men talked in the orchard, a small window in one of the turreted rooms flew open, the king leaned out and was heard to shout: '*I am murdered, this is treason*'.

The king's guards ran up the stairs and burst into the room where they came upon the sight of the Master of Ruthven and the king rolling around on the floor. Ruthven had a dagger in his hand; one of the king's men stabbed Ruthven in the neck and he was pulled from the king and finished off. The Earl of Gowrie who had run up the stairs with the royal guards was also killed. Another man in the room who was wearing amour and carrying a weapon turned out to be the Earl of Gowrie's chamberlain, Alexander Henderson, who did not play any part in the attempt on the king's life. Henderson claimed he had been forced into taking part in the attempted assassination by his master, the Earl of Gowrie but when faced with the reality of the attack could not harm the king.

The king's version was that once he and the Master of Ruthven got to the small room, instead of the black man, the king was expecting, there was Henderson in full amour, with a sword in his hand. Ruthven drew his dagger and told the king he was going to die for executing Ruthven's father. It seemed that the king had narrowly escaped an attempt on his life. But not everyone was convinced by the king's version of events. It took the king around a month to publish his account of the incident, and although four of Gowrie's servants were tortured and three hanged not one of them agreed with the king's version. The king was in debt to the Gowrie family to the tune of £80,000, a vast sum in these days, and the king was struggling to service the debt. The loan of course would be written off with the death of the Earl of Gowrie and his brother. In addition, because they had been involved in an act of treason, the Crown seized the Ruthven's lands and possessions. The only person who knew what really happened was Alexander Henderson, chamberlain to the Earl of Gowrie. We might have expected Henderson to be implicated for not coming to his king's rescue and stopping Ruthven attacking the king. Henderson however received no punishment. He was given lands and a pension by the king. (It has also been suggested that jealousy may have been a factor in the killing of the Ruthvens, the Earl of Gowrie being one of the queen's favourites.)

The bodies of the Master of Ruthven and the Earl of Gowrie were taken to Edinburgh where they were put on trial for treason. The two corpses were found guilty and taken to the Cross of Edinburgh where they were hanged, drawn, and quartered.

Three years later, James VI rode to London to be crowned James I of England bringing about the Union of the crowns of Scotland and England. He was to survive another plot on his life in 1605 when Guy Fawkes attempted to blow up Parliament – an attempt on King James's life that is famous and celebrated across Britain every November the fifth and an attempt at regicide no less important than the Gowrie Conspiracy.

* * *

CHAPTER TWO

The Bloody Inches

WILLIAM WALLACE

*Methven was surrounded by a great forest at one time, which
was used by outlaws and broken men as a place to hide out.*

TRAVELLING through Methven Wood would have been extremely
dangerous. During the Wars of Scottish Independence, the great Scottish
freedom fighter William Wallace used the forest around Methven as a
hideout and base. Like a real-life Robin Hood, Wallace would emerge from
the forest to hit at English military targets before disappearing back into
the dense woodland. Wallace had a fierce hatred for the occupying English
forces partly, according to the poet Blind Harry, because Sir William
Heselrig, the English Sheriff of Lanark, had killed Wallace's wife, Marion
Braidfute, in 1297. In retaliation, he and his men attacked and harried
them constantly. To the English ruling class, William Wallace was 'Public
Enemy Number One'.

When Wallace was in the Methven area, he would try to get to Perth
(St John's Toun as he would have known it), to meet a young woman of
whom he was very fond. One day, he decided to pay her a visit. He also
wanted to see how strongly the city was garrisoned. The English garrison
commanders knew Wallace was camped nearby, planning an attack, and
they were aware of his relationship with the local woman, so they hatched

Opposite: North Inch.

their own plan to capture the 'outlaw'. They told the woman they were watching her house day and night and she would be killed if she did not betray Wallace by lighting a candle by the window when he visited. The lit candle would be the signal for watching soldiers to storm the house and take Wallace. Fearing for her life, the woman reluctantly agreed.

A few days later, Wallace made his way through one of the heavily guarded city gates, disguised as a priest. After determining the strength of the forces holding Perth, he went to visit his lady friend. The English soldiers watching the house did not take much notice when they saw a priest enter the building but when the candle by the window started to flicker, they immediately went into action. Runners were sent to bring reinforcements. Back inside the building, the woman immediately realised what she had done and told Wallace of her betrayal. Aware that they did not have much time, the woman dressed Wallace in some of her clothes and after hiding a dagger in his undergarments, he fled the house.

As Wallace made his way to the gate at the southern end of Perth, he saw English soldiers in a state of high alert. Priests were being stopped, roughly disrobed, and searched. The soldiers manning the gate searched every cart leaving the city but somehow he managed to slip past the watchful eyes of the guards.

Relieved to be out of the city, Wallace started to run across the common ground that is the South Inch. Two guards on the gate spotted a tall, awkward looking woman running across the inch, and, shouting at her to stop, gave chase. They soon caught up with Wallace who struggled to run in female attire. One guard grabbed Wallace's shoulder and spun him around. For a brief second, the soldier stared, not into the eyes of a woman but a fierce looking man. Confusion spread across the soldier's face followed by feelings of pain and fear. He looked down, saw a dagger sticking from under his ribs, and his heart pumping blood over his assailant's hand. As the soldier's legs gave way, Wallace grabbed the dying man's sword. The other guard was still trying to register what had just happened when Wallace brought the sword crashing down onto his skull. Wallace then ran off and escaped, free to carry on his war with Edward I of England until his capture and execution in 1305.

* * *

THE BATTLE OF THE CLANS

The clans in the highlands of Scotland were an unruly lot. They were constantly feuding with their neighbours and regularly raiding into the low fertile lands of Moray,

PERTHSHIRE, Angus, Aberdeenshire, and Stirlingshire. The king's laws meant very little to this warlike, tribal society. In 1396, things were so bad between Clan Chattan and Clan Kay, who were forever raiding each other's lands, stealing livestock, and burning down houses, that King Robert III sent an army north to deal with the problem. The commander of this army knew it was likely that when he marched into the mountains, his forces were in danger of being ambushed by the men of Chattan or Kay – or perhaps both clans would unite. The outcome could be the massacre of the royal army.

So he came up with a plan and sent messengers to speak to the two warring clans with a proposal. This was a chance to sort out the problem in one day, sparing countless lives. The commander of the king's army suggested that the two clans each send thirty men to Perth for a fight to the death on the city's North Inch. The clan chiefs agreed and when the king heard of this plan, he was so delighted, he decided he and his court would come to Perth to watch the spectacle.

A large brightly coloured pavilion was put up for the royal party and benches were laid out for the people of Perth to sit on. The crowd waited expectedly in the warm summer sun as the skirl of the bagpipes drew closer and closer. Then dozens of kilted warriors took up position on the inch in front of the king's pavilion. As the two clans lined up, a referee counted the men on both sides but a problem was found. Although Clan Kay had thirty men, Clan Chattan had only twenty-nine. They must have miscounted before they left or lost a man on the way to Perth. Royal heralds walked amongst the crowd holding up a gold coin for anyone who would take up arms and fight for Clan Chattan. The city population murmured amongst themselves and fidgeted as the king, looking on like Caesar in the Colosseum, waited patiently. Just as it seemed no one would take up the offer of gold and Clan Chattan would have to forfeit the contest, a voice boomed from the benches: '*I Sir Herald will take that coin and fight for Clan Chattan!*'.*

The voice belonged to the city blacksmith, a giant of a man, strong and powerful. His name was Henry, better known as Hal o' the Wynd. Hal was given a sword and took up his place amongst the Chattan clansmen.

The king gave the signal to start and arrows were fired between the two sides. Then the men, screaming their clan slogans in Gaelic, charged into the affray. The sunlight danced on sword and axe blades as they cut through the air, slicing into flesh and bone. The green grass became crimson red and sticky from the flow of blood as the screams of the wounded echoed around the inch. The referee called a halt to the battle and the two sides parted. Sweating, panting men, soaked in blood, gulped at the water given to them and used it to wash blood from slippery hands. They likely used their few minutes of rest to glance around, looking for friends or kinsmen, counting how many were still alive compared to the enemy. Wounds were quickly patched up with strips of torn cloth before the signal to fight came again.

The two clans got stuck into each other once more. As the two sides slogged it out, it became clear that Clan Chattan were gaining the upper hand and in the end, all but one of Clan Kay perished. The sole surviving Kay jumped into the River Tay and swam to safety. Hal o' the Wynd was said to have fought bravely. He was permitted to keep the gold coin and earned his place in Scottish history.

(Previous page) Some accounts say the Battle of the Clans was fought between Clan Chattan and Clan Cameron.

THE FIRST PROTESTANT MARTYR

John Resby was an English priest who came north to Scotland to preach about new thoughts and practices involving religion.

NOT ONLY was the Pope's authority being questioned by new ideas, the belief that bread and wine taken at communion was the body and blood of Christ was being doubted. In addition, Resby did not believe in the worship of idols. These beliefs were fundamental to the Catholic faith. As Resby made his way around Perthshire, the Church heard of his inflammatory teachings so he was arrested and charged with forty acts of heresy.

In 1407, John Resby was found guilty and burned at the stake, probably on Perth's North Inch where people found guilty of witchcraft would later be burned. It is not hard to imagine Resby belting out hymns at the top of his voice from the pyre as the flames crept closer, safe in the knowledge that his soul would be saved. Then silence, apart from the crackle of the flames as they hungrily devoured their victim and thick black smoke, heavy with body fat, billowing across the inch. Resby was to be the first martyr in Scotland to a new faith, which was to sweep through Europe: Protestantism. After much bloodshed, the Protestant faith became the religion of most Scots.

A FAILED RESCUE ATTEMPT

Sir William Ruthven, Sheriff of Perth, led an expedition north in 1443. His mission was to bring a notorious thief from Atholl to justice.

THE FUGITIVE was apprehended and taken back to Perth to be hanged. John Gormac who was the head of a band of robbers assembled his followers and prepared to rescue the captured thief. This must have been done without sufficient time to plan or was poorly organised as there are many places in Atholl where a successful ambush could have been carried out. Mistakenly, the attempt to liberate the prisoner took place on Perth's North Inch. There both sides clashed. During the heavy fighting Gormac was killed along with thirteen of his men. Also amongst the dead was Sir William Ruthven. There is no record as to whether the thief was killed in the fighting or was indeed hanged on the gallows of Perth.

CROMWELL'S CITADEL

Shortly after the defeat of a Scottish army by Cromwellian forces at the Battle of Inverkeithing on 20 July 1651.

OLIVER CROMWELL himself rode in to occupy Perth. Many men from the Fair City had fought and died at Inverkeithing. After the Scottish defeat, Cromwell marched to Bridge of Earn and from there to Perth. When Cromwell's troops reached Perth, they found the city gates shut. John Davidson, who had survived the Battle of Inverkeithing, had taken command of the city defences and was determined to hold the city. Davidson ordered carts to be driven up and down the streets and drums beaten to give the impression that Perth was well garrisoned and capable of withstanding an attack. But Perth was in fact poorly defended, so the next day (22 August 1651) the city surrendered.

A few days later, Cromwell left Perth; a strong garrison under Colonel Overton with instructions to build a citadel (fort) in the city remained. This citadel stood around the spot where the Edinburgh Road meets Marshall Place (on the South Inch) and was so big it could offer stabling for 200 horses. One hundred and forty families were cast into the street as their homes were demolished to make room for its construction -the homeless becoming the responsibility of the council.

Building material was sought for the citadel, so the walls of Greyfriars Burial Ground were demolished and used. Over 200 gravestones were also taken. The builders robbed stone from the city hospital, Perth Grammar School, and the bridge across the River Tay. For the ramparts, they stripped the turf from the North and South Inches, denying the city much needed income from the grazing fees. The city was also responsible for supplying the troops garrisoning the fort with foodstuff and hay for the horses. It became a major expense for the people of Perth. As you can imagine, the citadel was not a popular construction!

This citadel was completed by 1652 and took the form of a low square fort, surrounded by a moat and protected by a rampart of earth and turf. It was occupied until shortly after Cromwell's death in 1658. According to George Penny in his book *Traditions of Perth*, the moat surrounding the citadel was filled in around 1780. Penny comments that it was at one time teeming with pike and in the winter boys would go skating there. Sadly, some of them fell through the ice and were drowned. He also mentions that unwanted infants were carried there under cover of darkness and cast into the murky water.

* * *

EXECUTION ON THE NORTH INCH

On the early morning of 24 August 1716, a 23-year-old soldier was led out onto the North Inch to the slow haunting beat of a drum.

THE MAN, John Knox, was sentenced to be shot by a firing squad for deserting the Duke of Argyll's army and joining the Earl of Mar's Jacobite forces. Knox was part of a Jacobite army that crossed the border with England, joined with an English Jacobite army, and marched to Preston. Knox was captured after the defeat and surrender of the Jacobites at the Battle of Preston, which had raged in the Lancashire town, 13-14 November 1715.

During the Jacobite wars, any government soldiers who deserted to join the Jacobite cause were shown no mercy if they were captured. John Knox was defiant and brave to the end as he faced his executioners, stating that in joining the Jacobite supporters of the exiled King James he hoped to relieve his native country of the oppression it was suffering. His last words before he was silenced forever were:

'*God bless King James*'.

DRUMMER BOY SHOT AT DAWN

During the Jacobite Risings of 1745-6, a regiment of government troops were quartered in Perth.

SOME OF THE SOLDIERS decided to go out to Scone to drink in the taverns there. They managed to persuade a young drummer boy to go with them. As the drink flowed, the young lad got talking to some locals who had Jacobite sympathies. These older men persuaded the drummer boy to join in a few toasts to Bonnie Prince Charlie and King James. This from a soldier in the government army was treason. But it was all a bit of a laugh and would be forgotten about in the morning.

The landlady of the tavern was a witness to the night's events. She got up early the next day and went into Perth to report the boy to his superiors. He was arrested and tried by court-martial. The boy was found guilty and his sentence was to be shot on the North Inch. He was taken to the top of the inch and duly executed at a spot known as the White Dykes. His distraught mother ripped off his bloody, bullet-holed shirt and took it to the tavern in Scone where she nailed it to the front door, beseeching God for vengeance. George Penney states that the lad was buried where he fell and a stone slab with a carving depicting a drummer boy could be seen there until 1793.

PRESS-GANGED

Being so close to the wild highlands, Perth has often been used as a military base from where troops could be sent quickly to any area that was giving the government trouble.

RED-COATED SOLDIERS were a common sight in the streets, which led to tension in the city. In the 1750s, things got so bad between the army and the populace that the military commanders decided something had to be done to improve relations with the citizens. It was decided to put on a grand review of the soldiers stationed in Perth. This would take place on the North Inch and all the dignitaries and common people of Perth were invited.

The soldiers in their bright red coats and highly polished buttons made dashing figures as they marched to the fife and drum. The Lord Provost took the salute when the troops marched past as the crowd cheered and waved. The soldiers formed lines and the garrison commander and provost walked slowly along the lines of troops, stopping now and again to utter some words of encouragement.

Everything was going well. The citizens were out in large numbers and seemed to be enjoying the occasion. Perhaps problems of the past could be forgotten and a fresh start made between the troops and citizens. The soldiers then started going through their drill as their sergeant barked out orders. Suddenly, there was a loud bang and the smoke from gunpowder rose slowly and hung in the air. A soldier had accidentally fired his musket and the ball tore into the crowd. A man, holding his young daughter in his arms, felt something warm and wet trickle into his hands. The musket ball had found a target and killed the little girl. As her father fell to his knees and those around looked on helpless, time stood still for a couple of seconds. The troops were the first to respond, they broke ranks and ran at the crowd. As the population turned and fled, the soldiers grabbed as many young men and boys as they could. They were dragged to the barracks and told they were to be pressed into the army. It took quite some time and diplomacy by the city officials to secure their release from the clutches of the redcoats.

REDCOATS EXECUTED

As we have seen, the military carried out punishments and executions on the city's North Inch but the army also used the South Inch to perform such vicious acts.

WILLIAM WILKINSON was shot on the South Inch in September 1754 for repeated acts of desertion. Perhaps one of the most distressing and inhumane acts committed by the military on their own within Perth took place on 7 January 1755.

John Hall and John Lamb served in Lord Robert Manners's Regiment, which was also known as the 36th Herefordshire Regiment of Foot. Both men had been tried and found guilty by a general court martial of deserting and each were sentenced to be shot on the South Inch.

A line of red-coated soldiers made their way to the execution spot to the slow death march of a beating drum. Among the red uniforms were the two condemned men in bright white shirts. When the party came to a halt, the prisoners knelt in prayer as the regimental chaplain took the service. It was recorded that Hall was particularly repentant. Suddenly, the officer in command decided that one of the men was to be given a pardon but with a cruel twist. The choice of man to receive it was to be decided on a roll of a pair of dice. He who rolled the higher score would be allowed to live. It is impossible to understand the stress and strain on both men when the reality of this offer sunk in. John Hall rolled his dice on the drumhead and it was a seven. Then, after spending some time pacing up and down while praying out loud (which must have done nothing for Hall's nerves) and in a highly tense atmosphere, Lamb rolled his dice. His score was an eight. At that, Hall fell to his knees and called for God to have mercy upon his soul. Lamb was taken back to the regiment and John Hall was shot dead.

The *Scots Magazine* of June 1755 states that John Lamb was again found guilty of desertion and he was shot on the South Inch on 30 May 1755 – only four months after being given another chance. Perhaps he never fully recovered from the stress of the events that took place in early January.

MURDER ON THE SOUTH INCH*

*One market day in Perth (in 1767), two soldiers,
John Chapel an Englishman and Duncan Campbell
from Ireland, noticed a farmer selling a lot of produce.*

THE TWO MEN kept a close eye on just how well business was going for the man. Once the market had finished the farmer made his way to a nearby tavern to have a few drinks before he started on his journey home. As he sat near the bar with his friends, the farmer told everyone just how well he had done that day while taking large amounts of cash from his pocket to buy drinks. He was unaware that he was being watched by two shadowy figures in uniform.

The farmer finished his drink, said his goodbyes, and staggered out of the tavern. He mounted his cart and headed out of Perth on the long road home. He did not get very far though, for as he made his way through the city's South Inch, two assailants set upon him. The two men pulled the farmer from his cart and as one held the farmer, the other man stabbed him in the stomach. The attackers then went through the farmer's pockets as he lay dying on the ground. They only got a few coins from the injured man and cursing their luck, they fled the scene.

The next morning, the farmer's body was found and a vital clue lay beside the corpse – a soldier's bayonet. People started remembering the two soldiers in the tavern who, although they sat quietly drinking, never took their eyes off the farmer and how they left just after him.

Chapel and Campbell were both arrested and executed for the crime. Their bodies were left hanging on the gibbet in chains, slowly rotting, and feeding the murder of black crows that haunted the execution site on the Burghmuir.

---

* This story refers to the two soldiers that city records state served in the 6th Regiment of Foot. A death warrant for them from 1767 orders that for the crime of robbery and murder, the two soldiers were to be fed on bread and water and when hanged their bodies were to be hung in chains upon the gallows. Although the document of the time refers to the men as both named Campbell, the Encyclopaedia of Scottish Executions, which records every execution in Scotland from 1750 until the last hanging in 1963, names the two hanged soldiers as Duncan Campbell and John Chapel.

BOYS WILL BE BOYS

*Some troops were engaged in carrying out a drill on the North
Inch. The soldiers were raw recruits and were being put
through their paces by their drill sergeant.*

AS THE MEN laboured through the drill, a group of young Perth boys
gathered and openly mocked the soldiers, pretending to charge at them and
then pretending to fall dead in front of them. This must have been very
annoying and off-putting for the soldiers.

The troops were practising loading and firing their muskets, which
were not loaded with shot. The troops fired a volley, a scream was heard
and as the smoke cleared, to their horror the soldiers saw a young lad lying
on the grass clutching his chest, his shirt blood red and his terrified friends
gathered around him. It seemed as if one of the soldiers had placed a musket
ball in his weapon and deliberately fired it at the boys. Upon further
inspection, it turned out that a soldier, in between drilling, had been
leaning on his musket, the barrel of the weapon sticking into the soft
ground. The barrel became clogged with gravel and soil and that is what hit
the boy on the chest. Luckily the wounds were superficial.

DISPUTE OVER PAY

*War broke out between a nervous Britain and France after the
French Revolution (1789-99).*

ANTI-ESTABLISHMENT and republican feelings swept across the English
Channel and those in power looked for signs of disobedience. There was a
feeling of public unrest in Perth, evidence of which became visible when the
citizens woke up one morning to find the bridge decorated in large chalk
letters and slogans:

'*Damn to all Kings, and Britain must be a Republic*'.

Two writers, William Wedderspoon and David Buist, were found to be
responsible.

Troops were raised for the war and to keep a watchful eye on the
people of the British Isles. Two troops of fencibles (regiments of mostly
local volunteers called up for service on home soil) were raised under the

command of Moray of Abercairney. The men had been recruited with a promise that their pay was to be two shillings a day, plus allowances. When, however, they were paraded on the North Inch and Graham of Inchbrakie read out the statement regarding pay, they were told that it would be sixpence a day plus allowances, bringing it only up to two shillings – a bit of a difference. Not surprisingly, the men were not too impressed. One of them cried out that this was gross deception and they would not stand for it. The captain, his face red with rage at this insubordination, ordered two corporals to seize the man. He was grabbed and frogmarched forward. Suddenly, the troops broke ranks rushed forward and freed the captive. The men were forced back into order with some difficulty and made to march up and down the inch. The captain gathered a body of dragoons (mounted troops), who made their way to the inch and arrested all the troops. The man who made the complaint about the pay received 700 lashes for his trouble.

AN OFFICER WHIPPED

A soldier who was struggling to feed his wife and four children was caught stealing some potatoes in a field. He was court-martialled and sentenced to 500 lashes on the North Inch.

A LARGE CROWD gathered to watch the man being punished. Before the whipping began, the man's wife, with her children in tow, approached the commanding officer and pleaded for mercy. This plea fell on deaf ears and the punishment started. The soldier bore the first few strokes of the lash bravely but as the punishment continued the man's skin began to rip, causing deep wounds. Seeing this, his wife put down her young child, who she had being carrying, and ran and grabbed the arm of the sergeant administering the whip. She was

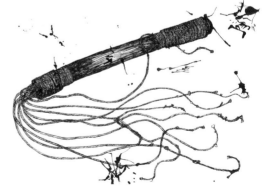

seized and dragged away kicking and screaming. The whipping continued. Some washerwomen in the crowd had seen enough and started to pelt the soldiers with stones. The citizens then rushed forward and overpowered the troops. The unfortunate prisoner was released and his wounds treated. The women then grabbed an officer and overpowered him. He was thrown face down onto the muddy ground, his trousers were roughly removed, and he received a thrashing with the cat-o'-nine-tails that had been used to whip the poor soldier.

MIDSUMMER MARKET

In the past, when they reached a certain age, orphan boys were sent from Perth into the countryside armed with a small box of needles, pins, lace, and the words of a few ballads.

WITH THESE, they were expected to make a living. After selling, swapping, and bartering, they returned to Perth to sell what they had acquired at the midsummer market. Stalls were set up along the city's High Street and in the evening these orphan boys fought pitched battles with local lads. Purse slitters and pickpockets would have a field day during the uproar and mayhem.

After the market, these orphan boys (known also as packmen) would meet on the South Inch and elect office bearers and representatives. When the official work was done, the entertainment started with horse racing and riding on a horse with a lance tucked underarm towards a target. The target was a hoop hanging from a crossbeam and the winner was the person who could collect the most hoops on the end of their lance. A barrel was hung up, inside this barrel was placed a live cat, and the barrel was filled with soot and sealed. The riders' objective was to break open the barrel with their lances. The one who freed the cat not only got covered in soot but also won a prize. The poor cat was tossed around the crowd until dead. It was said that one year when the cat was being thrown about, it landed on the head of a respectable lady's child who had been walking with his/her mother through the inch. The cat lashed out scarring the poor child for life.

* * *

27

A YOUNG LOVER LOST

One fine winter's day in 1867, a young draper's assistant named Robertson used his time off work to go for a pleasant stroll on the South Inch with his sweetheart.

THE COUPLE sat on a park bench beneath a clump of trees, chatting away together. Suddenly, without any warning, one of the big trees that had stood seventy feet tall and weighed around three tons came crashing down. It landed on top of Robertson killing him instantly. Workmen who had been in the process of removing it had weakened the tree, its roots had been cut and the earth at its base had been loosened. The three workmen who had been responsible for leaving the tree in such a dangerous state were charged with culpable homicide.

ASSAULT AND ROBBERY

Grace Douglas was charged with assaulting and robbing a man on the South Inch in July 1896.

THE MAN had been drinking all day and decided to sleep off the effects of the booze in the warm summer sun on the South Inch. No sooner had he dozed off when he was awoken by a group of women who demanded money. He handed over a few copper coins and then left for a quiet spot away from the women to get a bit of peace.

He had just settled again when Grace Douglas approached him and demanded more money. The man stood up and after refusing to give Grace any cash, pleaded to be left alone. A row broke out and Grace lashed out and struck the man knocking him to the ground. She sat upon the struggling man, proceeded to take his watch from his breast pocket, and remove the money from his pockets before making her escape. Unfortunately for Grace, she was caught and stood trial for the crime. Her sentence when found guilty was three months' imprisonment.

* * *

POISONED

On Friday, 23 October 1903, a man was seen acting strangely on the South Inch.

HIS NAME was Alex Nicoll, a former soldier who lived in Cross Street and worked as a railway surfaceman for the Caledonian Railway Company. He was sitting on a bench clutching his stomach, groaning, and seemingly in great pain. Some passers-by stopped and tried to assist Nicoll. A cab was hailed and Nicoll was taken up to the Perth Royal Infirmary. It was discovered that he had consumed a large amount of laudanum, a very addictive form of opium. It was then commonly used as a painkiller and to treat other maladies such as coughs, so it could easily be bought over the counter. Although the surgeon, Dr Parker, fought to revive him, Nicoll died later that day.

CRICKET DISASTERS

On the weekend of 31 July-1August 1903, a cricket match was held on the North Inch.

THE CONTEST was between Perthshire and Forfarshire and the stakes were high as they were playing for the Scottish Counties Championship. A vast crowd, estimated by some to be up to 10,000 people, turned out for the match, many of whom were day-trippers from in and around Dundee. A stand was erected for the occasion by a local firm of joiners, Thomas Leith & Sons. The company was experienced in building sporting stands and the 180-foot long structure, which stood on the North-East enclosure, could hold 1,100 people when full.

On the second day of the cricket match, the stand was around half full, many of the occupants being women. At five to three in the afternoon, without any warning, the stand toppled over, falling towards the cricket pitch. Those sitting in the rear of the wooden structure were catapulted over the seats in front. It must have felt as though time stood still for a few seconds as the stand seemed to come to a rest. A cry of *'jump'* could be heard as the people sitting in the first row of seats leapt onto the ground and away from the immediate danger. Then with a sickening crunch of splitting wood, the whole structure came crashing down. The collapse was described in the *Dundee Courier* (3 August 1903):

'*It fell with a frightful crash, carrying its human freight,*
many of them ladies, with a sickening thud to the ground'.

It did not take long for doctors, ambulance wagons, and cabs to turn up as news of the disaster swept through the city. A detachment of Black Watch soldiers arrived from the barracks to lend a hand. One soldier, Sergeant Major Preston of the Perth Royal Artillery, did a particularly good job of organising the construction of makeshift stretchers using cricket bags, jackets, and other things that could be found lying around. Thousands flocked to the North Inch as news spread, many fearful for friends or relatives who might have been caught up in this disaster.

As the victims were rescued from the wreckage of the collapsed stand, it became clear that although many were injured, some quite seriously, there were no fatalities. Many of the people hurt are best described as walking wounded. The victims' personal effects that lay scattered around were all gathered up and kept in the pavilion. The worst of the injured were 11-year-old James McDougal who lived at 282 High Street – he had suffered a fractured skull and a crushed chest – and James McEwen, a gardener from Monifieth, who had his right leg broken.

At the inquest in December 1903, the fault was found to be with Thomas Leith & Sons who erected the stand. There had not been nearly enough braces supporting the wooden joists. In fact, so few that some joists were completely unsupported while others had a supporting brace fitted to one side only when they should have been supported on both sides. Nails had been used to tie the battens to the uprights when bolts would have given much more strength and support to the structure. Thomas Leith & Sons were fined for negligence.

Ten years after the cricket stand collapsed, disaster hit the Perth cricket fraternity again. This time, the misfortune was no accident but the work of suffragettes who were fighting to obtain votes for women.

The pavilion of the Big County Cricket Club stood on the North Inch. All who were connected to the club would have been filled with excitement and apprehension as a new season was getting underway, despite the first match with Auchterarder being rained off. Around 7pm on Saturday 26 April 1913, the groundsman, Thomas Walker, locked up the pavilion. Everything was quiet when a patrolling policeman passed the pavilion at about 10pm but when Constable Alexander Keay was doing his rounds around Balhousie Avenue at 2am, he noticed the glare of a fire on the North Inch. Keay saw that the cricket pavilion was ablaze and raised the alarm.

By the time the fire services arrived, it was too late to save the wooden building as the fire was burning fiercely. Priceless Perthshire cricket memorabilia were destroyed by the fire: old photographs, trophies, and the club records. When an investigation was carried out, it was found that the fire had been started deliberately at the back of the pavilion. The suffragette movement was almost immediately blamed. A witness reported two women and a man acting suspiciously in Muirton Place earlier that night; and a couple of weeks before the cricket pavilion fire, suffragettes had unsuccessfully attempted to destroy the stand at Perth racecourse. Burning down sporting facilities was certainly within the *modus operandi* of the more hard-line suffragettes and they even sent letters to the cricket officials wherein they seemed to admit the burning of the pavilion at Perth.

With the outbreak of war in August 1914, most (but not all) suffragettes ceased their activities and rallied around to help with the war effort. Women finally obtained the vote with the passing of the Equal Franchise Act, 1928.

* * *

ERECTED BY
GEORGE CRAIGIE, *Flesher in* I[?]
AND
ANNA BISSET, *His Spouse*
IN MEMORY OF THEIR SON
THOMAS CRAIGIE
WHO DIED [?]OUT 1768
AGED [?] YEAR[?]
[?] ROBERT CRAIGIE
[?] JOHN CRAIGIE
[?] WILLIAM
[?] CRAIG[?]

CHAPTER THREE

Smuggling, Famine, Grave Robbers, and Witchcraft

THE GIN RUNNERS

Ever since tax was introduced as a way of raising money for the Crown, some people have resented their hard-earned cash being siphoned off by those in authority.

HOW OFTEN have you complained or heard complaints about the amount of tax on fuel for your car or how much tax comes off your pay at the end of the month?

People have always tried to obtain goods as cheaply as possible and one way of getting goods at a low price is to cut the tax man out of the deal. Smuggling was big business at one time in Perth. Smugglers were seen by the local populace as heroes, helping people avoid paying excessive or unjust taxes on everyday goods and essentials.

As Perth had its own harbour, the city was an ideal place to bring contraband into Scotland from abroad -thus avoiding the excise man. Around the late 1700s, Robert Faggo, a sailor, retired from a lifetime on the high seas decided to live in Perth and became involved in the linen trade. At one point, he had to visit London for business and whilst in the English capital, he met the master of a ship from Perth, which was docked there. The two men went for a drink and together came up with a moneymaking scheme. Their plan was to fill the ship with hogsheads (large barrels for

Opposite: Greyfriars Burial Ground.

transporting goods) of water, they would then add a top layer of hogsheads filled with beer.

The ship, laden with water and beer, would set sail for Perth – at least that is what they would tell the customs officers. Instead of heading up the coastline to Scotland, the ship would sail for the open sea and across to Rotterdam. In Holland, the hogsheads containing water would be emptied and filled with gin. The ship would then sail to Perth. When it reached Perth's harbour, the customs officials on checking the top layer of hogsheads full of beer would, of course, assume the whole cargo was also beer. This meant Faggo and his associate would pay the low tax on beer and not the much higher tax on gin. The hogsheads would be unloaded and with the top layer containing the beer removed, the more valuable hogsheads of illicit gin would be taken and spirited away, then sold to the grateful citizens of Perth at a knockdown price.

Vast quantities of goods were smuggled into Perth just like this, particularly gin from Holland and brandy from France. A lot of this spirit was stored in the garden of a boathouse, where Kinnoull Church now stands. The contraband was buried under vegetable plots by the old man who owned this boathouse. He made so much money from this illegal industry that he became a major property owner in Bridgend.

EXPLOSION IN COUNTY PLACE

At one time, the Ann Inn,* a tavern in County Place, was owned by Luckie Waterson. The inn was a popular drinking den with citizens and travellers alike.

THE MAIN REASON for its popularity was the cheapness of its drink. This was because Luckie was a regular customer of a group of smugglers who often brought goods into Perth harbour.

A ship had just supplied Luckie's cellars, which were full to overflowing with illicit liquor. Candle in hand, she went down to inspect her stock. Setting the candle on one of the wine racks, she counted the new delivery and worked out how much money she owed the smugglers.

Luckie then set off for the harbour to pay the men, leaving the lighted candle burning in the cellar that was filled with highly flammable alcohol.

Suddenly, a huge explosion shook the city and when the dust cleared the *Ann Inn* was nothing but a pile of rubble. Flames shot up high into the air and smoke billowed over Perth. Luckily, no one was killed.

* Another tavern situated on the High Street had the reputation of having the finest smuggled whisky in Perth.

FAMINE MEAL RIOTS

Between the early 1700s and the early 1800s, the crops regularly failed due to disease or the effects of bad weather, and the price of meal (grain) shot through the roof.

THE IMPACT on the population of Perth was that many were unable to afford staples like bread and oats. This shortage of food led to an outbreak of riots and public disturbances in many towns and cities throughout Scotland.

Empty carts appeared daily from Crieff, Auchterarder, and Dunkeld for meal as these places were also suffering but if a merchant was found to have supplied these carts with foodstuffs, he would often have his premises smashed up by an angry Perth mob.

On the night of 30 December 1772, with there being no meal for sale in the city for eight to ten days, a large group of people driven by hunger boarded a ship in Perth harbour and stole forty bolls (a wooden measuring bowl) worth of grain. The magistrates were unable to disperse the frantic crowd, so the military were called and the crowd broke up. For a while, all was quiet within the city but at three the next morning, the citizens assembled again. Faced with yet another day's hunger, desperate and unable to feed their children, they marched to the premises of John Scot, a baker. The mob smashed their way into his bakery and a large quantity of flour, meal, and bread was taken. Two of the mob were captured and locked up in the jail.

On the same night as the ship in Perth was looted, a vessel at Newburgh was also robbed by starving locals. With resentment and unrest breaking out not only in Perth but in the surrounding countryside, the magistrates realised things were becoming dangerously out of control and ordered the local farmers to send what meal they could spare to be sold to the public at the market in Perth.

On 2 January 1773, an angry crowd assembled. Their intention was to free the two men who had been captured and imprisoned. The magistrates called in the army to keep order and the soldiers placed cannons loaded with grapeshot in front of the council building. An official who read the Riot Act and demanded the mob to disassemble was pelted with stones. The soldiers charged the crowd with fixed bayonets and a violent battle raged around the Horsecross. The troops under a constant barrage of missiles and faced with angry locals armed with cudgels, pitchforks, and other weapons refused to stand guard any longer unless they were given permission to fire at the crowd. Fearing a bloodbath, the soldiers were ordered to withdraw by the provost. The two prisoners were then duly delivered to the mob which soon dispersed, satisfied.

Rumours began to circulate around the city that a farmer, John Donaldson, at Elcho (a village about three miles south of Perth) had a quantity of grain. Hearing that Donaldson was in Perth at a local wine merchant, an angry crowd made their way to the vintner's establishment but failing to find the farmer there, the mob proceeded to Elcho. Despite a body of ten soldiers guarding John Donaldson's house and granaries, the mob entered Donaldson's home and obtained the keys to where the grain was stored. The keys were taken back to Perth and presented to the deputy sheriff. The mob angrily demanded of him that John Donaldson be made to bring in his meal to be ground and sold in the city.

As the lack of food continued, a starving population who were rationed to one loaf of bread a week took to scavenging for scraps for sustenance. Old dunghills provided bones and rotten vegetables that could be made into a soup. Soup kitchens were set up, long queues of hollow-eyed, gaunt and weak men, women, and children lined up for a bowl of thin stew made from boiled cow heads and barley.

CANNIBALISM IN THE FAIR CITY

In 1332, a Scottish army surrounded the city.

HOLDING OUT against them were a force of Scots and English troops loyal to Edward Balliol, an English backed rival for the throne. The Scots stopped supplies coming into the city and as the siege dragged on the population began to starve. With no food and all the city's animals (including dogs and horses) devoured, it was said the populace resorted to eating grass. But there was one man who did not look like he was suffering, a man who looked to be gaining weight and appeared to all to be quite fit and healthy. His name was Andrew Christie.

Imagine you were there in the streets of old Perth, doubled over from the pain of hunger, desperate for something to eat. Christie might come up to you and whisper in your ear that he had some food and would share it with you. You were instructed to go to his house when it was dark and remember to keep it to yourself, do not tell anyone as he only had enough food for the two of you.

As night fell and the streets became quiet, you would use the little energy you had to scuttle to Christie's house. Once there, he would sit you down and tell you he was going to prepare your meal. But you were in a very dangerous situation because Christie had not invited you for dinner – you were his dinner! He had turned into a murderous cannibal. Christie would· kill his victims and consume their flesh. Eventually Christie was caught and hanged for his crimes. He is remembered as Christie of the Cleek.

For generations after, local parents warned their children that if they didn't behave, Christie of the Cleek would get them!*

---

* There are a few variations of this story: one is that he was a Perth butcher who fled the city with his family and they lived in the hills where his murderous clan would ambush travellers, kill and eat them; another says that he was not hanged but he did make a deathbed confession.

THE GRAVE ROBBERS

At one time, Scotland had the best medical schools in the world.

STUDENTS FLOCKED HERE to learn medicine in the great schools of Edinburgh, Glasgow, and Aberdeen. But there was a problem: in the days before X-ray machines, the only way to see how a body worked was to get one and cut it open to have a look inside. As medical schools were only allowed the corpses of hanged murderers, demand always outstripped supply. Men who were known as Resurrection Men, Bodysnatchers, or Sack 'em up Men would break into graveyards at night and, with hushed voices and black cloth wrapped around two-thirds of their lanterns, dig up a freshly buried grave with wooden shovels. These grave robbers would dig a narrow hole at the eastern end of a grave – Christians are buried facing east – where the head of the body would be until they hit the lid of the coffin. They would break open the coffin, place a rope around the corpse, and haul it from the grave. It was big business, as many medical schools would pay between £7 and £10 for a body.

In 1723, a surgeon, James Smith, and nineteen others connected to the medical profession were said to be involved in lifting Ann Asplen from her grave in Perth. The following year, the council was forced to pass an act fining anyone caught stealing bodies from Greyfriars Burial Ground £20, with a reward of £10 to informers. Surgeons' apprentices would be fined £5, whipped, and put on the city pillory if they were caught lifting the dead.

MOB VENGEANCE

A wright (carpenter or joiner) had decided to supplement his income with a bit of nocturnal grave robbing. Soon, word leaked out and spread through the city.

A LARGE CROWD assembled and marched to the man's house. As he was nowhere to be found, the crowd trashed his home. Not satisfied, they marched to his workplace. Again, he was not there, so the mob smashed the place up and on leaving took the wright's business sign. This was taken to the main gate of Greyfriars Burial Ground and nailed to a tree as a warning to anyone else who might fancy a bit of grave robbing.

A YOUNG BRIDE TAKEN

A young bride, who was obviously very unhappy, drowned herself in the River Earn.

HER BODY was buried but a few days later someone noticed that it had been stolen. Her elderly uncle made his way to Perth, with the sole intention of finding the body of his niece. No one held much hope that the sad old man would succeed but the weavers of the city took pity on him and organised help. Soon everyone was involved in this search and the girl's body was found hidden in a disused malt barn. It was wrapped in a plaid, laid over a horse, and taken solemnly to her uncle.

DASTARDLY DOCTORS

Dr Drysdale was from Perth and it was said he was implicated in the lifting of a body from Scone in 1820 but the case against him was dropped.

THIS IS PROBABLY related to an incident that is recounted by Robert Scott Fittis, a prolific Victorian writer on all things Perthshire, in his *The Weavers Records of 1888*. In this account, an indictment was taken out against a James McGregor, a doctor living in Edinburgh, and John Walker who at the time was a prisoner in Lanark. McGregor had been in the employment of two surgeons, John Smith and William Ramage, also from Edinburgh. They were alleged to have lifted the body of James Taylor who worked as a forester for the Earl of Mansfield at Scone Palace. Taylor was buried at Old Scone Cemetery on 15 October 1820.

At about midnight on 22 October, John Mason, a chaise driver for the *George Hotel* in Perth, was hired by a gentleman guest to pick him up at Bridgend. At the Scone Road junction, the driver was met by the gentleman who was accompanied by another two men. One of the men had a trunk tied to his back. The trunk was placed into the chaise, the men climbed in, and asked the driver to take them to Kinross and then on to Burntisland, Fife. It was there that the body of John Mason was discovered and identified.

Another doctor who lived in Perth's Tay Street was thought to have a dissecting room in his basement and would receive bodies taken from the graveyard at Kinnoull, which were then ferried across the River Tay. A close off the Watergate was locally known as Resurrection Close because it was home to a couple of known body snatchers.

* * *

WITCHES

In the latter part of the sixteenth century, a new danger befell Scotland: the Church and State were under attack from witchcraft.

GRIM LOOKING ministers encouraged people to be ever vigilant as evil was to be found everywhere. James VI was also involved and took a keen interest, blaming witchcraft for trying to sink his ship as it returned from Denmark with his new queen. He accused a group of witches in North Berwick of tossing a live a cat into the sea and thus casting up terrible storms that almost sank his ship.

Women who had in the past been considered healers or wise women were suddenly in grave danger – and it was funny how a wee bit of torture could loosen their tongues and implicate others. Hysteria swept through Scotland until the 1720s; and like every other town and city, Perth suffered this madness.

PERTH'S WITCHES

In 1580, the Kirk Session ordered a witch to be banished from the city. Two years later, on 12 February 1582, a woman living in the Meal Vennel was imprisoned in the Tolbooth for being a witch.

SHE WAS STILL incarcerated on 16 April; as records detail, it was decided to commit eight-twelfths of a penny for her keep, after which she was probably banished. By 1582, the days of casting a witch out from the city were very soon to be over. The punishment for anyone found guilty of witchcraft was almost always burning at the stake. In Perth, this was done on the North Inch. Christian Stewart was interrogated for three days in the Gowrie House in 1596. She was accused of using witchcraft and sorcery, involving a black clout (cloth), to kill Patrick Ruthven. She confessed and was sent down to Edinburgh to be tried. She was found guilty and burned on Castle Hill in the capital.

On 23 November 1597, the Kirk Session ordered the magistrate to travel to Edinburgh and obtain a commission to execute a woman accused of sorcery. Her name was Janet Robertson and she had been a long-term prisoner in Perth. It is thought that she was burned along with fellow alleged witches Marion Macause and Bessie Ireland, on 9 September 1598.

THE 1623 BURNINGS

In 1623, three women were accused in Perth of witchcraft.

THESE UNFORTUNATE SOULS were Margaret Hormscleuch, Isobel Haldane, and Janet Traill. (There is quite a lot of information regarding the trial of these three women in the Kirk Session Register.)

Margaret Hormscleuch confessed to curing John Hay who was in his sick bed at home in Logiealmond. Hormscleuch paid him a visit and after rubbing him in pig fat, she washed his body in water taken from a south running burn (a small stream or river). (South running water was a feature in many witchcraft cases.) Hormscleuch also cured Alexander Mason's wife, who was very ill, after asking that south running water be brought from the River Tay. She requested of the person who fetched it not to speak to anyone on the way to get the water or on bringing it back to Mason's house and that the mouth of the pig or jug had to be held to the North. Hormscleuch washed the woman with this water and then bathed her in meal. The patient made an immediate recovery and was said to be so well that she sat up and had something to eat with Hormscleuch. She also cured a woman in Muirton and restored milk to a cow in Ruthven.

At her trial, a dark side to Hormscleuch was discovered. When John Jackson, son-in-law of Margaret Kinloch, killed a sow that belonged to the accused, it was said that she cast a curse that affected Margaret Kinloch's health and that of her daughter. In another incident, when she asked a brewer, Hugh Pherskin, for a jug of his newly brewed beer and he refused, Hormscleuch turned away and mumbled something under her breath. Just then, a container full of beer fell and smashed on the ground followed by another five. Later, Pherskin, on passing Hormscleuch, heard her say some words and soon after was hit by an illness that lasted almost six months.

Isobel Haldane stated during her trial that whilst lying in bed she was taken by either God or the devil to a hillside that opened and she entered. There, from Thursday to Sunday, she was entertained by the fairy folk.

She made mention of a man with a grey beard. It was there that she learned how to heal people. Haldane cured Andrew Duncan's child after washing the infant with south running water. When she had finished, she took the water and the bairn's sark (under shirt) but on her way to dispose of the sark and water she spilled some. Haldane was to say that this was a terrible mistake because if anyone had stepped in the spilled water they would have become infected with the disease of which she had cured the child. In another accusation, it was said that Haldane gave David Morris's child a drink containing leaves from locally picked plants, unfortunately after drinking the liquid the infant died.

It seems Isobel Haldane was also able to divine the future as she told Margaret Buchanan, who was fit and healthy, to prepare for death. The poor woman died a short time later, probably scared to death by the warning. Hearing that James Chrystie was making a cradle for his soon to be born child, Haldane told him not to bother, as the infant would never sleep in it. She said that the child would live long enough to be baptised, then it would die. Sure enough, the baby died without sleeping in its new cradle.

Janet Traill, who was also accused of witchcraft, claimed that while at home in Dunning she was taken from her house by fairies. Some of them were wearing red, some grey, and all were riding horses. The leader, a bonny white man, told her to speak to God and be good to poor people. She cured a child in Ruthven and was known to be a close associate of Isobel Haldane.

The three women were all found guilty and sentenced to be burned at the stake on Perth's North Inch. Big crowds gathered to watch the terrified women die. The minister, filled with self-rightness vigour and confident he had defeated Satan's messengers, read the scriptures. He gave the condemned another chance to confess before God who had long since deserted the sobbing women.

The women's crimes were simply healing the sick and trying to help their neighbours. Yes, Margaret Hormscleuch might have been angry at the killing of her pig and cursed the man responsible, and yes, she might have been fuming at not being given beer by Hugh Pherskin and walked away muttering under her breath but that is all of which she was guilty – being

The burning of Margaret Hormscleuch, Isobel Haldane
and Janet Traill in Perth, 1623.

a bit crabbit and showing anger. The people who had asked the women for help were made to repent in public by having to dress in black cloth and on Sunday attend church and stand under the bell ropes. As the service started, they would then come into the building and sit at the front for all to see as the minister reminded everyone there about the crime they had committed.

Occasionally, sense prevailed. For example, in 1589 John Watson accused Guddal Wilson of being a witch. She was arrested and charged but it seems that instead of the usual torture with sleep deprivation or pricking her flesh with long pins to find the devil's mark, the views of her neighbours were asked. Everyone stated that they would never suspect her of witchcraft and they thought that she was an honest woman who looked after her sick husband. Wilson was released and allowed to return home while her accuser John Wilson and his daughter Helen were found guilty of slander.

The last two people found guilty of witchcraft and burned as witches in Perth were Margaret Ogilvy and Sarah Johnston (in 1715). The last woman burned at the stake for witchcraft in Scotland was Janet Horne in Dornoch (in 1727).

* * *

CHAPTER FOUR

War on the Streets

A HERO KING

Perth changed hands many times during the Wars of Scottish Independence.

AS PERTH occupied a key strategic position, holding the city was vitally important to both the Scottish patriots and the English invaders with their Scottish allies. On one memorable occasion in the winter of 1311, Robert the Bruce was besieging the city. He soon realised that Perth was well provisioned and stoutly defended, so withdrew his forces. King Robert lay low for a few days, then one moonless night returned with a few handpicked men. Silently, Bruce led the way as they slipped into the moat that protected the city. The waters were deep, coming up to the king's chin and, being winter, ice cold. The men that followed carried rope ladders with hooks on one end. Once they were all safely across the moat, the ladders were secured to the top of the city wall. Bruce and his men scaled the wall, quickly and quietly overpowered the guards, before opening one of the city gates for the rest of Bruce's troops to pour into the city. A French knight who had watched the scene reported to the king of France that he could not believe just how 'hands-on' Robert the Bruce had been in the capture of Perth.

* * *

Opposite: The Salutation Hotel.

RUTHVEN Vs CHARTERIS

In 1544, Patrick Lord Ruthven, a Protestant, was elected provost of Perth.

CARDINAL BEATON, Archbishop of St Andrews, aware that Ruthven supported the Reformation, wanted the Catholic John Charteris of Kinfauns to be provost instead. Beaton had Ruthven dismissed from office and replaced with Charteris. The burgesses (city officials) of Perth and most of the citizens supported Ruthven who refused to step down and barred the city gates. Charteris supported by Lord Gray and Clan Leslie decided to force their way into Perth. Charteris's men would attack across the bridge with one force, while another stormed the South Port (southern gateway to the city). Early on the morning of 22 July 1545, Kinfauns and Lord Gray moved their troops in silence up the northern bank of the river as the Leslies moved towards the South Port. As Kinfauns and his men filed across the bridge, the city was deadly quiet. It looked like they had taken the defenders by surprise but Ruthven's men had taken up concealed positions, hiding in buildings and down side streets. As the attackers entered the city, they were suddenly under fire from all sides. Panic and confusion gripped the men in the smoke-filled streets as no cover could be found. The troops attacking the South Port were also driven back. At the end of the firefight, between twenty and sixty of the attacking troops lay dead in the streets with many more wounded. John Charteris had his forces withdrew and Lord Ruthven remained provost.

ST JOHNSTONE RIBBONS

In May 1559, the Protestant reformer John Knox preached in St John's Kirk. His sermon was very anti-Catholic.

AFTER KNOX had left, a Catholic priest stood up and prepared to say Mass. A young lad complained that after Knox's sermon why were they were now being subjected to this. At this show of insolence, the priest struck the boy who fell to the floor. The lad picked up a piece of masonry and hurled it at the priest. This was enough to spark a riot. The congregation, their hearts aflame with passion and John Knox's words still ringing in their ears, smashed up all the holy statues in the church. Then they made their way through the city attacking all the religious houses of Perth. Fine historical buildings, hundreds of years old, were set ablaze, their priceless treasures lost. As God's buildings in the Fair City burned, the holy men and women fled to Stirling. There they informed the Regent, Mary of Guise, of the outrages being committed in Perth. The deeply religious and Catholic mother of Mary Queen of Scots was furious at what had taken place. She vowed to march upon Perth, burn the city to ashes and then sow the site of the city with salt so nothing would ever grow there again.

Mary of Guise and 8,000 troops, including a large body of French soldiers, marched to Auchterarder and set up camp. At Auchterarder, Mary was informed that the Protestant Earl of Glencairn had entered Perth with reinforcements and it looked like a large-scale battle was on the cards. Worried officials from Perth stepped in and, after a lot of negotiation, agreed to let Mary of Guise and her army march into Perth unopposed.

Mary's troops filed into Perth and up the Watergate, which was crammed with onlookers. As she passed, her French guard fired a volley in salute. On a crowded staircase, trying to get a good view was the 10-year-old son of the Laird of Tibbermuir. When the guards fired into the air, a musket ball hit the young boy and killed him. News of this tragedy was brought to Mary of Guise and knowing that the Laird of Tibbermuir was a friend of John Knox, she rather cold-heartedly said:

'It was a pity it chanced the son and not the father'.

Mary marched out of Perth leaving 600 Scots soldiers, who were in the service of the king of France, to hold the city. Foreign troops garrisoning the city was against the treaty. Although it was pointed out that these men were all Scots, the fact they were being paid by the king of France and were wearing French uniforms, meant they were regarded as French troops.

Lord Ruthven, the provost, decided to liberate Perth from these occupying soldiers, so he placed gun batteries to the west of the city. Protestants were now flocking from all over to help force the French out. The provost of Dundee and a large party of Dundonians held the northern bank of the river and placed their artillery to cover the bridge. Ruthven's guns opened fire on the city, quickly followed by those of Dundee. The garrison fired back killing one of Ruthven's men but before the attackers could return fire, a white flag was raised. The French troops were permitted to march out of Perth with their colours flying, in regimental order, and unmolested.

When news reached Mary of Guise as to what had befallen her men in Perth, she prepared to march on the city once more. The citizens prepared for the attack: some 300 men volunteered to defend Perth. Each man placed a noose around his neck and stated if they did not fight to the death to defend Perth then they should be hanged. These ropes became known as the St Johnstone Ribbons. Thankfully for the people of Perth, Mary gave up on her quest to take the city and headed instead to Dunbar.

* * *

FAMILY FEUD

Scotland's various families and clans often feuded with each other, which sometimes led to violent clashes when the lords and chiefs gathered for a parliament.

IN THE SUMMER of 1607, the government was scheduled to meet in Perth. Lords and ladies with their entourage of retainers and clan chiefs with their bodyguards flocked to Perth – the city was bursting at the seams. One night, the Earl of Glencairn and his men were making their way up the High Street. Passing on the other side of the street was Sir Alexander Seton and his followers. There had been bad blood between these two families for some time. As the two factions passed, their leaders tried their best to keep them apart but as you can imagine, the two sides began snarling at each other, chests were puffed out and some strutting took place. At the rear of the groups, some servants started to hurl insults across the road. A fight erupted and soon everyone was involved. In the mêlée, a few from both sides were injured and one of Glencairn's party was mortally wounded.

RICH KIDS MISBEHAVING

On 12 August 1618, George Lundy, Guthrie of Kincaldrum, and George Graham, son of the Lord of Claverhouse, had been drinking all day in the taverns of Perth with their friends.

AFTER THE PUBS closed, they made their way noisily and full of good spirits to their lodgings. Swords were drawn and no doubt a couple of them drunkenly pretended to have sword fights. They then decided it would be fun to cut down the market stalls that were there for the market the next day. At the same time as these shenanigans were taking place, John Mathew was passing with his servant boy. It might have been that John had an altercation with the group of drunken vandals or perhaps they just did not like the way he looked at them. Whatever the reason, they attacked John Mathew and the boy. The Common Bell was rung, one of the Perth bailies was called and he demanded that they stop their attack and go to bed. The drunken louts then turned on the bailie, tearing off his coat and severely beating him with sticks.

A BOXER KILLED IN THE HIGH STREET

At one time it was common for bareknuckle boxers to travel from town to town. They would erect a ring and challenge local lads to a boxing match.

THIS INCIDENT was said to have happened before the year 1740. One of these fighters set up his ring at the bottom of the High Street. He then issued a challenge to a match, offering a lot of prize money to anyone who beat him. If you accepted the challenge you had to enter the ring and kick the head of a drum, then the fight would take place in front of a vast crowd of excited onlookers.

Just as it looked like no one was prepared to fight the man, John Burt from Perth climbed into the ring and kicked the drum. The two fighters squared up to each other, and then the fight started. It was by all accounts a hellish contest as the two boxers pounded each other. Both men had terrible wounds to the face and head and were covered in blood and sweat. Feverish betting on the eventual winner took place as the two in the ring slugged it out. Burt swung an almighty punch, which connected with the other man's head, his legs buckled, and he collapsed onto the floor. This did not knock the man out – it killed him outright.

JACOBITES UNDER SIEGE

In late summer of 1745, Prince Charles Edward Stuart (Bonnie Prince Charlie) landed on the north-west coast of Scotland.

HE HAD COME to put his father James VIII of Scotland (James III of England) on the throne. Wearing the crown down south was George of Hanover who had been crowned George II. To the Jacobites, German Geordie or the *Elector*, as he was known, was an imposter king, King James being the true monarch. The prince gathered an army in the Highlands and marched south.

Prince Charlie's Jacobite army took Perth on 4 September 1745. Perth was divided between those who supported the Stuart cause and those who remained loyal to George II and his government. John Burt, who owned what is now the *Salutation Hotel*, was a keen supporter of the Stuarts. When Bonnie Prince Charlie rode through Perth at the head of his army, John Burt came out and publicly saluted the prince as he passed, hence, as the tale goes, the name *Salutation Hotel*. The *Salutation* at the time was an important coaching inn and the prince took rooms there during his time in Perth. Tension grew in the city as civil war gripped the land. A local man, John Rutherford, was so angered by those who did not bow to the prince as he rode out of Perth, that he grabbed some of them and violently threw their hats into the gutter.

When the prince left Perth to capture Edinburgh and invade England, he left a small force to hold the city. Conflict erupted in Perth on 30 October 1745, which was King George's birthday. Anti-Jacobite supporters rang Perth's church bells to honour their king. When ordered to stop by the Jacobite deputy governor, Lawrence Oliphant of Gask, the bell ringers defiantly refused and stated they would continue to ring the bells in honour of King George until ten o'clock that night. As the pro-Hanoverian supporters grew ever bolder, a big bonfire was lit in the street, again to celebrate King George's birthday. The population of the city were told to light a candle in their windows for the king. Those who did not had their windows smashed by a now very large mob but those who did had their windows smashed by the city's Jacobite supporters.

The Jacobite soldiers tried to restore order by firing into the crowd. They succeeded in killing and injuring a few of the assembled throng but this only led to a full-scale riot. The rioters overpowered the soldiers and marched to the Jacobite headquarters. A gun battle erupted in the streets as King George's supporters took pot shots at the Jacobites who were now barricaded in the building.

As the streets echoed to the sound of gunfire and filled with smoke, one of the Jacobite defenders of the besieged building, a French soldier, was shot through the head. A minister came forward and offered the Jacobites terms if they would surrender but this was refused. As the fighting continued, a messenger seeking assistance for the besieged Perth garrison arrived at the home (just outside Perth) of Lady Nairne, who was a staunch supporter of Bonnie Prince Charlie.

Lady Nairne gave all her staff a white cockade (a white ribbon worn on a bonnet to show Jacobite allegiance). Nairne's servants gathered all the available weapons that could be found and marched on Perth. The pro-government supporters must have heard that Jacobite reinforcements were heading to Perth, for when Lady Nairne and her domestic staff arrived in the city, the streets were quiet and the fighting had stopped.

It must be said that the population of Perth who took arms against the prince's troops that night showed some courage. The prince had taken Edinburgh and had also defeated a government army at the Battle of Prestonpans (21 September 1745). The Jacobite army was preparing to invade England and at that time it looked very likely they would be joined by a great number of English Jacobites and reach London unopposed.

In fact, although the Jacobites did invade England, they only got as far south as Derby before turning around and retreating to Scotland -due to lack of English support. Perth remained under Jacobite control until the Jacobite garrison withdrew in February 1746 to join the retreat north. King George's son, the Duke of Cumberland, finally and brutally crushed the Jacobite dream on the blood-soaked moor at Culloden on 16 April 1746. After the Jacobite defeat, Cumberland issued a proclamation to the people of Perth, warning that any person who hid any rebel, arms, goods, or ammunition belonging to the rebels would hang. The council, as a show of loyalty, gave the Duke of Cumberland the gift of Gowrie House. The Duke must have been a bit underwhelmed by this. As soon as he returned to London, he sold his new property to the Board of Ordnance who converted it into artillery barracks.

* * *

CHAPTER FIVE

The Black Death

HELL ON EARTH

In the 1340s, a new and deadly disease came to Scotland and unleashed hell on earth upon a terrified population.

ORIGINATING in the East, it travelled to Europe along the trade routes. Like a black cloud of death, it spread through England and was brought to Scotland by an invading English army – so initially the Scots called the disease '*the foul death of the English*'. It quickly became accepted that the pestilence killed indiscriminately and was brought down on mankind by a vengeful God as punishment for sin, or so it was thought.

There were two ways of spreading what became known as the Black Death:

Bubonic Plague is carried by fleas on rodents, most commonly rats, which lived hand in hand with humans in those times of poor sanitation. If you were bitten by one of these fleas, you could become infected. Once infected by bubonic plague, you would quickly start to develop flu-like symptoms, followed by swelling of the lymph glands. Large buboes (pus-filled boils) would appear in your groin area, under your arms and on your neck. These buboes eventually burst. Seventy-five per cent of those infected developed blood poisoning causing them to die about a week after their symptoms first appeared.

Pneumonic Plague spreads more easily from human to human than

Opposite: Kinnoull Hill.

bubonic plague, as particles of blood can travel up to four metres through the air when an infected person coughs or sneezes and two metres when someone with the disease is speaking. Pneumonic plague also spreads more effectively in cold and damp climates like Scotland, and is much more deadly than bubonic plague. Symptoms are manifest as early as a day after becoming infected. Initially, you have trouble breathing, then you develop a fever and a cough. Soon blood from your lungs begins mixing with your saliva and after two or three days you fall into a coma. Ninety-five per cent of those who caught pneumonic plague perished. On the bright side, those who survived the plague acquired immunity from the disease.

THE BLACK DEATH IN PERTH

Imagine that this weekend, you hear early on Saturday morning that a couple at the bottom of your street have been taken to hospital.

AN HOUR OR TWO later, you hear that three other members of their family are also reportedly sick. Then by evening, their neighbour has come down with this illness and a family two doors down from you have been affected. By Sunday morning, there are cases springing up all over; and by Sunday lunchtime, the authorities have restricted all movement in and out of the city. People are starting to die a horrible death, coughing up their own lungs, before slipping into a coma and dying. If this only affected a couple of hundred you would still be terrified, fearful for your loved ones. Now imagine this disease kills one-third of the population and rapidly spreads to other towns and cities. Everything you hold dear, your faith, your family, and the society you live in would never be the same again.

The Black Death frequently found lodgings in the Fair City. As the inhabitants of Perth succumbed to the disease, the council struggled to cope. Houses that were affected would have a piece of white cloth nailed to the door and a cart would make the rounds at night – the stillness of the evening broken only by a sad, lonely bell to tell you that you could now bring out your dead. Once full, the cart would be taken to one of the plague pits on the outskirts of the city, where loved ones would be unceremoniously tossed into a mass burial pit, covered in quicklime, and buried. Their possessions and clothes would be burned and their money cleansed in boiling water.

In 1348, the plague killed about a third of the population of Perth. It was said that in 1645, Perth was almost depopulated as over 3,000 men, women, and children were taken, turning whole areas into virtual ghost towns. Society's moral rules started to break down.

In 1538, during one outbreak, three priests and two citizens were prosecuted for breaking into and robbing houses where the inhabitants had succumbed to plague. They were also charged with assaulting the gatekeepers so they could escape with their loot. In 1585, orders were given for a couple to be carted backwards through the city wearing paper hats on their heads. Then they were to be locked in irons at the market cross and forced to stand there from 2-3pm. Afterwards, they were to be put in prison until Sunday where they would be taken to a church wearing their paper hats and made to sit on stools of repentance. The couple's crime: they had both survived the plague and whilst the rest of the population were involved in fasting and praying they were out celebrating this new lease of life by partying and enjoying each other's body. Quite understandable really!

THE AUTHORITIES HIT BACK

Perth council brought out a series of measures to combat the spread of plague.

IN 1585, a law was passed declaring that during a time of plague there should be no banquets at weddings and a £10 fine was to be levied on anyone who ignored the edict. In addition, anyone found guilty of fornicating would be required to pay a fine which would then be given to the poor affected by the plague.

In 1608, all communication with places infected with the plague was banned. Watchmen were placed at the city gates to prevent anyone from entering or leaving without sanction by the magistrates. Shanty towns were built on the South Inch, at Friarton, and on Kinnoull Hill, to which the infected and their families were sent. The dead were buried in pits at St Leonards. Foul Clengers (cleansers), who were usually people who had survived the plague, were sent into houses affected to clean them. The cleansers wore protective leather suits that had a long snout filled with

sweet smelling herbs for protection against the foul air that was believed to cause the disease. This gave them quite a sinister appearance. For this task, they received thirteen shillings. Infected houses were shut up and no one could enter except the physicians and cleansers. People who had been infected and recovered had to wear a white cloth on their breast for forty days. Dunghills were cleared and animals within the city were butchered.

BRAVE JAMES VI

In 1585, James VI was in Perth when the city was hit by an outbreak of plague that eventually killed 1,427 citizens.

DESPITE restrictions on travel from places where there was an occurrence of plague, the brave king fled the city and headed for Stirling. He ordered his servants not to follow him; four of them were to die from the Black Death in Perth. The good king also ordered the destruction of all bridges spanning the River Forth as a further precaution. Despite all these precautions, it was said to have been a maidservant from Perth who took the plague to Edinburgh that year, causing widespread devastation in the capital.

BESSIE BELL AND MARY GRAY

In 1665, a young girl, Bessie Bell, was living in Perth.

HER FATHER heard that plague had broken out in the countryside and was heading towards the city. He ordered his young daughter to go and live with her uncle's family at Almondbank. Bessie made her way to her uncle's home and was quite happy as she got on well with her uncle, aunt, and cousin Mary Gray. It wasn't long before Bessie's uncle heard that the plague had not only taken a grip in Perth but was starting to affect the villages outwith the city. He told Bessie and Mary that they must go and live away from any human contact – in the woods by the River Almond for their own safety.

The two girls built a shelter in the woods and lived happily on nuts and berries. One day, they got a visitor, Bessie's boyfriend, who lived in Perth. The young lad had missed her so much that he had decided to find her. After much searching, someone told him of two young girls living in the woods by the river and there he found Bessie. When Bessie saw her beau, she was overjoyed, she had missed him so much. No doubt he told Bessie and Mary of the news from Perth: how the plague had affected the city; who had died and who still lived, including news of Bessie's family. Then the lad went into his bag and brought out a present for Bessie. It was a silk handkerchief. She was delighted.

After spending most of the day with the girls, the boy stated that he must return to Perth, for his family were still living there. He kissed Bessie and made his way home. A few days later, Bessie Bell started to feel feverish and extremely ill. She had caught the plague. Mary nursed her cousin until she died but by now it was clear that Mary herself was not well and she also succumbed to the Black Death.* It seems Bessie's boyfriend had taken her gift, the silk handkerchief from the body of a plague victim, and that is what had infected Bessie who in turn infected Mary.

---

* *The site where the two girls died is marked by an iron enclosure around a yew tree beside the River Almond.*

'THE END?'

As improved hygiene and sanitation led to the slow demise of
the Bubonic Plague, with outbreaks taking fewer and fewer
*lives, the threat by the 'King of Killers' came to an end.**

IT WAS NOT REALISED at the time that a cleaner lifestyle was the cause. People simply thought that the plague had been rounded up and eradicated. One theory was that a Kincardineshire wizard had collected it in a golden pot and buried it. Another belief, more local to Perth, is that it was interred in the old Collegiate Church at Methven. A story goes that years after the last outbreak, two men were looking for treasure in the ruins of the church. Suddenly, out of the earth, rose a blue mist and a warning voice told them to stop digging or they might unleash another hell on earth.

----

* *Although in 1900 Glasgow suffered an outbreak of bubonic plague which killed sixteen people, plague in Scotland is now a thing of the past. The Black Death however still exists in some parts of the world – a terrifying spectre still capable of striking fear into the hearts and minds of mankind.*

* * *

CHAPTER SIX

The City Ablaze

FIRE

*Perth, like many other medieval cities, was confined by the
walls that were built around it for protection from attack.*

PERTH had walls to its south, east, and west; the north of the city was
protected by the River Tay. In those past turbulent times, Perth could not
spread outwards as a city, so it had to spread upwards. Timber framed
buildings, several stories high, packed together with residents cooking on
open fires, was a recipe for disaster. This was witnessed most famously in
the Great Fire of London of 1666, which started in a bakery in Pudding
Lane and devastated the English capital. There was also the fire of 1824 in
Edinburgh, which destroyed much of the Old Town – the fire's flames spread
rapidly along the rooftops of Edinburgh's old tenements.

Perth was also affected by sporadic outbreaks of fire that caused
widespread devastation. Unfortunately, it would have been near impossible
for the people to contain these fires, even as they worked in relays with
buckets of water from public water pumps. In one account of an attempt to
tackle a fire in Perth, a young woman died from exhaustion whilst
repeatedly carrying water, which speaks volumes.

* * *

Opposite: Murray Royal Hospital.

High Street Ablaze

In 1765, a fire broke out in the High Street of Perth.

IT PROPAGATED rapidly and engulfed properties as it travelled. The flames would have risen high into the sky; smoke would have been visible for miles and sparks from the burning buildings would have ignited more fires that would have had to be dealt with.

The 1765 fire devastated the High Street between Meal Vennel to the South (where the High Street entrance to St John's Shopping Centre is located) and Guard Vennel (the vennel adjacent to Skinnergate) to the North. In the aftermath of the fire, nine charred bodies were dug from the smouldering ruins of the buildings.

Leonard Street Fire

The sky above Leonard Street was illuminated by fire in 1777.

DESPITE the best efforts of the city's fire brigade, the fire moved rapidly, destroying six buildings. An old, bed-ridden man, who could not escape his home in time, died a horrific death, trapped and alone.

Bridgend Blaze

George Penny tells of a fire that took hold of a building in Bridgend in 1788.

HE STATES that a debtor looking out of his prison window in the Tolbooth at the bottom of the High Street saw smoke pouring from the building. Unfortunately, before he could summon help, the blaze took hold and seven people were killed. It appears that Mr Penny was incorrect as to the year: the *Caledonian Mercury* newspaper printed on 16 May 1793 tells of a fire in Bridgend. The paper declares that at the time of going to print six people had been killed, a man, two women, and a mother with her two boys. She had escaped but when out in the street noticed her two sons were still in the building. She ran back in and tragically she and her sons were lost. One man, who had escaped by climbing onto the roof, slipped and fell. He was not expected to recover. If the man did indeed die that makes seven dead, so it seems Mr Penny's story is correct but that he made a mistake with the date.

* * *

Salutation Hotel

The Salutation Hotel is the oldest hotel in Scotland and has played a role as a coaching inn since 1699.

AT ONE POINT in its history, a maid was killed in a fire in a large house that now forms part of the hotel. Again, in the early 1800s, there was a fire – this time in the hotel's stable block. Grain was stored in the ground floor of the building and the upstairs was used as a store for the army. This posed a real hazard, as along with general military stores were a few barrels of gunpowder. If these exploded, the explosion might have devastated the whole area. The fire brigade struggled to contain the fire and it quickly became apparent that it would spread to where the barrels of powder lay. A butcher, Robert Fenton, rushed forward and entered the burning building. Braving the intense heat and fumes from the smoke, he made his way to the upper storey of the stables. Grabbing the barrels of gunpowder, he rolled them to a window and then proceeded to throw them into the street. This act of bravery carried out by Robert Fenton saved Perth from disaster and perhaps great loss of life.

The George Inn

In 1816, the stables of another of Perth's old coaching inns, The George, caught fire.

THE FIRE SPREAD so rapidly that twelve horses were roasted alive. The noise of the commotion in the street as the blaze was tackled and the heart-wrenching noise of the poor animals trapped inside the burning building must have been awful. It would have been enough to wake the heaviest of sleepers, or so you might think. No, it seems not. A hotel resident sleeping in the room above the entry to the stable block slept through the whole event and was reportedly surprised when told about the tragedy at breakfast the next morning.

Murray Royal Hospital Destroyed

At about 11.30 on the morning of the Tuesday 9 May 1837, the distinct smell of smoke drifted up Perth's South Street.

NO DOUBT the citizens took note of this smell and discussed it; the consensus was that perhaps some broom bushes were being burnt upon

Kinnoull Hill. The burning smell seemed to get stronger as the day wore on but it wasn't until 1.30pm when the bell of St John's started to ring backwards, the alarm toll, that people realised something was amiss. It turned out that for the last few hours a fire had been smouldering in the roof space of Murray Royal Hospital.

The fire crews made their way to the hospital, as did a large crowd from Perth – said to be a few thousand strong. By the time they got there, the fire had taken hold, thick black smoke billowed up into the air and the flames could be seen dancing in the sky above the roof. A reporter from The *Perth Constitutional* painted a vivid scene:

> '*The loud incessant crackling of the combustion, the splitting of the beautiful Welsh slate, the falling of the rafters, the running to and fro of the attendants and others through the wards, to save as much as possible of the valuable moveables'.*

The 74th Regiment of Foot was brought in to help fight the fire, which with the help of a strong breeze had devastated the new wing at the back and much of the old main building. The patients, or as one newspaper unkindly refers to as the '*lunatics*', were all rescued. Some of them were seen to dance around seemingly taking much delight from the mayhem around them, while others stood and looked on quite indifferent to the events taking place.

At the end of the day, the damage to Murray Royal Hospital, which in 1837 had only been open for ten years, was evident. It lay as a smoking empty shell. The cost of repairs eventually ran into many thousands of pounds. While the Murray Royal Hospital was repaired, the hospital's patients were housed in the old French POW prison on the Edinburgh Road.

A Fireman Drenched

At 6.30pm on 6 December 1881, a fire broke out in the City Mills in West Mill Street and was discovered by one of the men working there.
THE FIRE, aided by a strong wind, quickly took hold. The fire brigade arrived quickly and started to tackle the blaze. They were soon joined by 140 soldiers of the Black Watch. Despite the best efforts of the firemen and

soldiers, by nine o'clock the building had been completely gutted. As the firemen tackled the fire, large crowds gathered. One wee boy slipped and fell into the Lade. He was swept downstream but luckily got caught in a grate and was plucked to safety. One soldier who had been fighting the fire, decided to take a break and have a smoke of his pipe. Probably fatigued, he momentarily forgot he was standing at the edge of the Lade. He decided to walk to the wall facing him to strike his match, took a step forward, and disappeared into the darkness – plunging into the water with a loud splash. His comrades, who thought the whole thing hilarious, pulled him safely out of the water.

Fire at Railway Blacksmith Shop

In November 1891, a fire broke out at the Caledonian Railway Company's gas works and blacksmith shop in Perth.

THE RAILWAY COMPANY used gas to light their carriages and it was stored in a building located just to the south of the station. Before leaving for the night, the foreman went to fetch something. When he returned, he found the building on fire. Unable to tackle the fire himself, he called for assistance. The railway company's fire brigade, along with the Perth brigade, and the firemen from the city's army barracks, tackled the fire. The firemen were hampered by a shortage of water as the area's water supply had been cut off due to work being carried out by the council. As the inferno blazed, the roof of the building collapsed causing a massive shower of sparks to fly high into the air. The collapsing burning roof timbers resulted in two gas boilers exploding sending deadly, white-hot razor-sharp metal shrapnel flying in all directions. James Bailas, a young ironmonger, who had been helping the firemen, was hit by some of this flying metal which severed his right leg below the knee. His hands and face were horrifically burned in the explosion and he died in the infirmary a few hours later. James Bailas was only twenty years old.

* * *

Council Buildings Destroyed by Fire

At around 3am on 23 January 1895, Superintendent Buist noticed sparks coming down the chimney of the Police Office, which formed part of the council buildings at the bottom of the High Street.

HE SENT for a chimney sweep to inspect the flue but by the time the chimney sweep arrived, it was clear that the chimney was indeed ablaze and had spread to the roof space of the building. The fire brigade arrived but the water pressure was too low and the building too high to tackle the fire effectively. The blaze spread through the roof and took hold of the rest of the upper stories. Documents were hurriedly taken from the council offices and put for safekeeping into the post office. The fire spread to the fine wood-panelled Commissioners Hall, where priceless paintings and windows depicting Robert the Bruce taking Perth from the English in 1311 and scenes from Sir Walter Scott's *Fair Maid of Perth* were lost forever. Flames also devoured the Burgh Court Room and Police Office.

At 4am, the roof collapsed, sending a shower of sparks and flames high into the early morning sky. The chief constable, his wife, and their seven children, who had a house in part of the building, were rescued from the blaze. The chief constable had time to get himself dressed but the rest of his family were led out the burning building distressed and shivering, wrapped in blankets. When the fire was eventually extinguished, it became clear the building had been gutted and the cost of repair would run into thousands of pounds.

A Mother's Agony

At noon on 18 February 1903, Catherine Wilson left her home
at 9 Cross Street. She was going to her husband's workplace with
his dinner.

AS SHE LEFT, she locked the front door. Inside the flat were her three children, Catherine Wilson aged four and her two brothers, 3-year-old William and Thomas who was a baby of seventeen months. The morning had been cold, so a fire had been set and lit in the grate. Shortly before one o'clock, a neighbour noticed smoke escaping under the door. The locked door was broken down and once inside, the room was found to be full of smoke and ablaze. The fire brigade were called and when they arrived, the fire was quickly put out. It seems a coal had fallen from the fire and ignited the bedclothes in the room. Two of the children were dead and a third although unconscious was brought round. The agony and guilt felt by Catherine Wilson when she discovered what had happened at Cross Street during her absence can only be imagined. She was arrested two days later at her mother's house in Guard Vennel, charged with causing the deaths of her two children, and was sent to prison to await her trial. The *Dundee Evening Post* (11 March 1903) records that the charges against Catherine Wilson were dropped. Perhaps it was decided that the loss of two children was suffering enough.

* * *

Perth Theatre Fire

As George Cushney, a well-known junior footballer in Perth, walked to his work at the Perth Tramway Department around 7am on 29 April 1924, he passed Perth Theatre in the High Street, where he noticed smoke billowing out from some of the windows.

CUSHNEY ran off to raise the alarm, and within minutes Perth City Fire Brigade were on the scene. As the firemen busily went about their tasks, Fire Chief William Patterson immediately realised that if the main doors were opened, it would create a through draught which would fan the flames in the burning building. Patterson ordered that the doors remain shut and that access to the theatre interior was to be from the windows at the rear and side of the building.

Hoses were directed at the blazing floor and roof of the upper dress circles. As the fire raged, it soon became clear that the water from the street hydrants was not going to be enough to quench the flames, so Patterson ordered one of the engines to pump water from the Lade at Mill Street. The hose from this engine was taken up Cutlog Vennel and through the stage door. It was then fed across the stage, up a staircase, and the water was directed at the upper dress circles where the fire raged. Within half an hour the fire was brought under control.

There was extensive damage to the upper part of the theatre. It seemed that the fire had started in the third tier of seats in the upper circle. The cause of the blaze was a dropped cigarette, which had been left to smoulder all night. The fireman employed by the theatre inspected the premises at 10.30pm and found nothing amiss – even though the cigarette must have been smouldering then. The upper circle and the dress circle in front were completely gutted by the fire, which had damaged the ceiling and spread to the gallery (which was only slightly damaged).

Although the cost of the damage was estimated at being between £3,000 and £4,000, it could have been a lot worse if it had not been for the experience and professionalism of William Patterson. By not allowing his men to open the main doors and thus causing a draught to flow through the building and fan the flames, he saved the stalls, the pit, and stage, as well as the dressing rooms behind, from being destroyed.

• • •

CLOTHING CATCHING FIRE

In the days before fire resistant materials, when everyone warmed their homes with open fires, accidents and deaths caused by clothing catching fire were common.

Family Hit by Tragedy

In 1844, the grandson of Mr Anderson, one of Perth's shoemakers was killed when his clothes ignited.

ACCORDING to the *Dundee Courier* (31 December 1844), it seemed that the tragic death of the youngster was only one of a number of accidents to befall the family. The paper detailed that within a three-week period, one of the young boy's sisters broke her leg after falling from a cart; a brother was melting some candle wax when he spilt some onto his mother's hand, which was so badly burned it looked as if the hand might be lost; the same brother was badly hurt when some boys sliding down a ladder landed on top of him – his cheek was cut to the bone; a second sister, on the day of her young brother's funeral, fell asleep by the fire and was badly burned; and a grandfather had burned his hands so badly while trying to save his granddaughter that he lost the use of them. This was a family that did not need to go searching for trouble.

An Old Lady Engulfed by Flames

In 1849, an old man went to church, leaving his aged wife in bed.

ON LEAVING the house, the man locked the door and took the key with him. His wife got up and went to stoke the fire, her nightdress caught light, and soon she was engulfed by flames. With the door locked, she was unable to escape and when the alarm was raised the locked door hampered any rescue attempt. Sadly, by the time entry was gained to the house she was dead.

Children Set Ablaze

In 1879, a young boy died in his home in the High Street when, whilst standing by the fire, his clothing caught fire.

A FEW YEARS before that, in 1866, two passers-by were met with a horrific sight in South Street when a 4-year-old girl, Mary Malone, who had been left home alone ran into the street in a ball of flames. Luckily, the horrified onlookers managed to extinguish the fire. This also happened in 1928 when 16-year-old Rhoda McKay was in the kitchen of her home at 8 Pomarium Street. She was looking after her mother who was confined to bed. Rhoda was cleaning out the fire. As she stood up, her dress came into contact with a gas hob that was lit. Immediately her clothing caught light but Rhoda was unaware of this, until warned by her mother who had witnessed the garment catching fire. In a blind panic, she ran out into the street as the flames engulfed her. Duncan McLean who lived in the same street as the stricken girl ran to her assistance and wrapped her in a rug, smothering the flames.

Workplace Dangers

At the end of May 1907, a young maid, Joan Reid, was busily carrying out her tasks at the home of her employer
STEPHEN RICHARDSON, a music teacher who lived in Atholl Street. Joan was cooking at an open fire when a cinder fell from the grate and landed on her skirt. In an instant, her clothing caught fire and flames engulfed the poor woman. The other domestic servants rushed to her aid wrapping her in a rug to extinguish the flames but she had terrible burns and was taken to hospital in a critical condition. She died a few days later.

On 13 December 1912, a 20-year-old Glaswegian kitchen maid, Kate Goudie, at the *Grand Temperance Hotel* in Perth was working in the kitchen when her dress caught fire. The *Dundee Courier* of Monday 16 December, stated:

'Her sunny disposition made her a great favourite!'.
The paper also claimed that Kate succumbed to her injuries.

* * *

CHAPTER SEVEN

The Merciless Tay and Other Watery Perils

LIVES LOST

Perth has witnessed some tragic accidents over the years and the River Tay has claimed its fair share of victims.

THE DROWNING of three young boys in the river on the afternoon of Monday 18 April 1870, was such an accident and one that shocked the city. Eight boys had taken a boat out and were '*messing about on the river*'. They decided to pass underneath Perth Bridge, despite the river being high and the current under the bridge being especially strong. Three of the youngsters objected to this dangerous action and were dropped off on the bank at the bottom of the High Street. The other five foolhardy boys rowed towards the bridge. It seems that they were almost underneath the bridge when one of the oars struck a rock and snapped, which caused the boat to turn into the current. The frightened boys all rushed to one side of the boat and it capsized throwing them into the raging torrent. Some onlookers tried to help but there were no lifebuoys to hand, so the struggling youngsters had to wait until a boat could be launched. Two of them, Francis Davaney and David Alexander, were plucked from the water. They were the lucky ones and were taken home to recover. It soon became clear that it was now no longer a rescue but a search for bodies. Hundreds of silent onlookers lined the foot of the High Street as the river was dragged. James Methven's body was found

Opposite: Perth Bridge over the River Tay.

below the council buildings. The following day, 11-year-old Alexander Mitchell was found near what is now the harbour. A day later, a boy referred to only as Nicol was found two miles downstream. It was decided that because of this tragic accident lifebuoys would be placed along the riverbank.

Bridgend Woman Swept Away

Even going about your everyday business was hazardous near the River Tay, for the river when in the mood took no prisoners.

JESSIE FERGUSON, a 24-year-old woman from Bridgend was filling a pitcher with water from the river on 8 January 1882, probably something she had done many times before and without much thought, when the Tay claimed her life. As she was collecting the water, she either lost her footing and slipped or was overcome with dizziness and fell into the water which was fast and deep at that point. She was swept away to her death.

* * *

Perth Lade

The River Tay was not the only body of water in Perth where lives were lost.

THE LADE, once part of the defences of Perth before supplying the industries of the city with water, runs right through the city. The Lade has also claimed its fair share of lives. On the morning of Sunday 13 November 1887, a policeman found the body of postman Robert Reid from Huntingtower in the Lade near Balhousie. It was thought Reid had been out the night before and had fallen into the water on his way home. When his body was pulled out of the Lade, his watch was found to have stopped at 10.50pm giving a good indication as to when the accident happened.

A miller, George Graham, whilst going to work at 6am on Saturday 7 October 1899, discovered the body of a woman floating in the Lade. She was later identified as being Susan Haggart, who on the Friday night after finishing her shift as a cleaner at the Caledonian Road School, went to get some shopping. She was never seen alive again. Apparently, the poor woman slipped and fell into the Lade and was drowned.

Three Young Lives Sadly Taken

On 23 July 1888, John Harris was walking on the North Inch when he heard the screams of a young boy who had paddled too far out into the River Tay.

HARRIS and two other passers-by ran to the boy's assistance but were horrified to see the youngster disappear before their eyes under the rapid-flowing water. There had in fact been three young boys playing at the river's edge. They were trying to reach sticks that were being washed downstream by a flash flood caused by a recent thunderstorm. A crowd of some 4,000 people congregated on the North Inch as the river was searched. Many parents were unsure if it was their children who were missing. At the side of the water, a cloth cap, two pairs of boots, and two pairs of stockings were found, the initials DK were sown into the cap. The cap belonged to an 11-year-old boy, David King, who had been out playing with his 9-year-old brother, Bruce, and their friend, 11-year-old James Spiers. Tragically, all three boys were drowned.

* * *

A Lucky Escape

In the afternoon of 15 May 1890, two young couples decided to rent a boat from a Mr Dutch who ran a boat hire business on the North Inch.

IN ALL LIKELIHOOD, the two young women sat at the back of the boat while the young men rowed the vessel up the river. As they steered the boat into the Sawmill Stream at the top of the North Inch, it was caught in a fast-flowing current and capsized. The four youngsters were thrown into the cold water. Luckily for them, a passing sailing boat, the *Vera*, picked up the two women and one of the men. The other young man managed to swim to the riverbank and for once the Tay was denied its prey.

Rowing Team Drowned

On 15 August 1895, five young members of Perth Rowing & Sailing Club decided to go onto the river to practise for an approaching regatta.

DESPITE it being the middle of summer, there had been a lot of rain and the river was swollen and fast flowing. To the cries of the coxswain, the rowers made their way up towards Perth Bridge. It would seem they misjudged the force of the notorious bridge current. The boat was spun around by the ferocious strength of the bubbling water, which left the front of the boat pointing towards Bridgend, side on to the power of the downstream current. The boat capsized and the crew were tossed out into the wrathful river. A crowd looked on helplessly as the men fought for their lives. One of them attempted to swim upstream against the current but his strength gave way and he disappeared under the merciless water. Another made his way to the island opposite Bridgend but on seeing one of his companions struggling tried to help and was carried away to his doom. Another two were seen to be in serious trouble by onlookers at the foot of the High Street. A small rowing boat (belonging to two local fishermen) picked up one of the men who was floating face down in the water. He, the 16-year-old coxswain, Robert Allen, the youngest of the rowing team, was the only survivor. The dead were James Galloway, a dyer, George Fleming, a hammerman (both residents of Perth High Street), Charles McQuhae, a blacksmith from St John's Place, and James Kay, a dyer who lived in Union Lane.

A Father's Nightmare

Wednesday 27 June 1917, was a nice sunny summer's day in
Perth; the first for a while as there had been a lot of rain earlier
on in the month.

A LOCAL BUTCHER, John Frew, who lived at 31 Rose Crescent, decided to make the most of the fine weather and took his three daughters out on a boat on the River Tay, whilst his wife took a trip on a steamer to Dundee for the day. The family made their way up the river in a small rowing boat and the girls were having a great time, perhaps waving and being waved at by the people walking along the riverbank. As he rowed into the entrance of the Sawmill Stream, John Frew's boat got caught in the fast-moving current and capsized. Frew and his two elder daughters managed to grab hold of the upturned boat but Frew was horrified to see his youngest, 3-year-old Dorothy, being swept away by the current. Although he could not swim, Frew made a valiant effort to save his daughter, managing to grab hold of her clothing twice but both times she slipped from his grasp and was swept away, lost to the river.

Died With His Boots On

One of the most unusual drowning accidents on the River Tay took
place on 28 December 1919.

A BODY was discovered at low tide at the bottom of the pier at Perth Harbour. It was James Cameron, a 56-year-old fencer, who resided at 5 Meal Vennel. He was standing upright in the water and was stuck in the mud. The man who spotted the body of Cameron, about ten feet from the side of the pier, was a labourer, George Younger, also from the Meal Vennel who was walking down at the harbour. Cameron's corpse was standing, bent forward slightly, in around five feet of water; and although he was 5' 11" in height, at high tide he would have been completely covered with water. Younger and a fisherman, David Stewart, managed to pull the stricken man from the water using a boathook. The corpse was wearing a watch, which had stopped just after midnight, suggesting the time of drowning. Cameron's body was taken to the mortuary and identified by his wife. Just why James Cameron was standing in the mud at the harbour remains a mystery.

* * *

For a Lost Ball

*The mighty River Tay can be utterly heartless at times and no
more so than on Saturday 3 November 1923, when young Charles
Thornton Wood, the 12-year-old son of Charles Wood who ran a
fruit and confectionary shop and lived at 38 High Street, went
into the river to retrieve a miskicked football.*

CHARLES usually helped his father in the shop on a Saturday but that day
his father let the young lad go to play football on the North Inch. During
the game, it was reported that a passer-by booted the ball into the river.
Charles went to fetch the ball and was seen wading out into the river to
retrieve it. He was only a couple of feet into the water when either he
stepped into a deep pool or lost his footing, and disappeared under the
surface. A young woman from Dundee was visiting her friend in Perth.
The two ladies were on the North Inch and witnessed Charles fall in. The
Dundee lass ran towards the river, then in the direction of the old bridge
where Charles was struggling in the water. The women rushed along the
riverbank looking for a lifebuoy and when they found one they ran down
Tay Street calling for assistance. A man took the lifebuoy and threw it at
Charles but it landed just out of reach. Another young boy, the same age as
the drowning boy in the water, Evan Ferrier of 61 High Street, ran with a
second lifebuoy down the steps opposite the *Royal George Hotel* and threw it
at Charles but again the throw was short. A short time later, Charles
Thornton Wood disappeared under the water. As the crowd gathered and
looked on helplessly, two of Charles's friends arrived with his cap and jacket
thinking their young chum would be cold when taken from the water and
would need them to keep him warm. The fact that witnesses watching
stated that almost immediately after Charles had fallen into the river, his
football came ashore at the exact spot where the boy had entered the water
makes this such a tragic accident.

* * *

CHAPTER EIGHT

Accidents

GUILDHALL COLLAPSE

In the later 1700s, plays were regularly performed in the Guildhall.

ONE NIGHT during a run of *Macbeth*, the wooden gallery in the hall that was packed with 300 people came crashing down. In the mayhem of dust, splintered wood, and fallen masonry, many were trapped and injured. As the news spread through the city, travelling from mouth-tomouth, the tragic story grew arms and legs. For although many people were hurt, no one was killed but the news that spread like wildfire through the streets was that many people had died. Vast crowds of concerned citizens flocked to the Guildhall, all expecting the worst. There was great relief when, finally, word came that there had been no fatalities.

BOYS WILL BE BOYS

Two young lads stood fishing at the spot where the Lade flows into the River Tay on 25 September 1865.

THE TWO FRIENDS were James Campsie a 19-year-old dyer, and James Gibson who was fifteen years of age. It seems that the younger lad was teaching the older how to fish, as he was the one casting off both lines.

Opposite: PerthRailway Station.

The weights were stones tied onto the fishing line. Gibson prepared to cast off. As he swung the fishing rod back, the stone became loose and flew backwards through the air like a bullet. It hit James Campsie on the head just behind the ear. Campsie fell to the ground unconscious, blood flowing from the wound onto the ground. A doctor was quickly brought to the scene but there was nothing that could be done. James Campsie was dead, a result of a freak accident.

BOATYARD SHED COLLAPSE

At one time, boatyards operated on the banks of the River Tay at Perth and many fine vessels that went on to sail the seven seas were constructed in Perth.

ON FRIDAY 8 October 1869, one of these vessels was due to be launched, a 550-ton clipper, the *Cottica*, which had been built for Messrs Adam Pearson & Company, Glasgow, to trade with the West Indies. A large crowd gathered to watch the launch of the ship; many of them congregated in a disused shipyard next door to the one where the *Cottica* had been built. Lots of folk stood on and around an old shed by the water's edge – on the roof of which were perched a great number of children, while the adults sat underneath. Just as the *Cottica* was launched and slipped into the water, the shed collapsed due to the weight of those on the roof. Two children, a boy and girl were thrown into the River Tay but luckily they were quickly pulled out from the water. Some of the youngsters on the roof were seriously hurt, as were some of those sitting underneath. A Mrs Puller of Scott Street broke her leg, as did James Mathewson of Canal Street when in the uproar his leg became entangled in the chains connected to the *Cottica*. A young boy, David McFarlane, received severe back injuries. Many others received minor wounds (mostly cuts and bruising).

* * *

NEAR DEATH BY THE TRACKS

In the early hours of Sunday 4 May 1878, an old man, John Campbell, who was a fireman employed by James Calder & Son Wood Merchants and who lived at Friarton, was making his way home along the railway line at the Friarton siding.

CAMPBELL fell near the railway track and could not get back up – perhaps he had a wee drink in him or simply could not see properly in the dark. As he lay on the ground, a train passed by, the wheels went over John Campbell's hands almost severing one so that it was only held on by a loose piece of skin. The other was so badly damaged it had to be amputated in hospital. The wheels passed so close to the old man's head that a portion of his hair was sheared off.

DEATH IN SOUTH STREET

Great excitement was felt at teatime on Monday 21 September 1885 in Perth's South Street, as a slow moving agricultural traction engine gradually made its way down the street.

CROWDS gathered to watch and the machine was followed by a large group of excitable children who were trying to clamber on board the engine. Eight-year-old Archibald Taylor was one of a number who climbed on the engine and once on board enjoyed the ride down the street. Unfortunately, young Archie slipped and fell, he hit the ground right in front of one of the traction engine's wheels, which went over his head killing him almost instantly. The owners of the engine, William Anderson, were charged with culpable homicide for having failed to provide a person to prevent children climbing aboard the traction engine as it passed through Perth.

* * *

FREED PRISONER KILLED

Mary Love, an outdoor agricultural worker, had just been liberated from the General Prison at Perth (29 September 1897) after serving a 14-day sentence for breach of the peace at her lodgings at Newton of Pitcairns.

SHE CELEBRATED her freedom by getting drunk, then decided to make her way home. Luckily, as she stood at the railway bridge on the Edinburgh Road, she saw a cart approaching. The cart was being driven by Hugh McKay and was loaded with aerated water. Mary stumbled out in front of the cart and demanded a lift. Hugh McKay, seeing the woman was intoxicated, refused to stop, so Mary was forced to step aside and let the cart by. As it passed, she jumped on to the vehicle, grabbing at the tarpaulin that covered the crates of water but the tarpaulin had not been tied down and slipped, allowing Mary to fall backwards between the horses and cart. Before the shocked driver could pull up, the cart had passed right over the body of Mary Love. She was taken up to Perth Royal Infirmary where she died from her injuries.

MESSENGER BOY SHOOTING

When James Frances of South Street met his young friend, Thomas Kerr, a message boy who lived at Thimble Row, on 19 December 1902,

THOMAS could barely hide his excitement as he had something to show James. Thomas Kerr proceeded to take out a six-chambered revolver that his father had just bought and he had managed to smuggle out of the house. As the two lads toyed with the gun, there was a loud bang and James Frances gave a cry of pain. The five chambers on show were clearly empty but an unknown bullet in the sixth chamber over the barrel had been released when one of the boys pulled the trigger. The shot tore into Frances's left thigh. He was carried into a shop in George Street and then to hospital. Inspector Scott of Perth City Police was soon on the scene. He found forty-four bullets in Kerr's possession and the very distressed young message boy was taken into custody.

WORKPLACE ACCIDENTS

The workplace was often a hazardous site and it was not unusual for workers to be seriously injured, maimed, or even killed as they went about earning an income.

A Young Girl Crushed

Two joiners were busy repairing a gate at the entrance to a house in Bridgend on 29 July 1874.

THE MEN, William Rutherford and his son, had just erected half the heavy wooden gate when they decided it was about time they stopped and had some breakfast. Before they left, the two men propped up the gate with wooden batons. A large group of children were playing nearby and once the workmen had gone, their curiosity got the better of them so they ventured over to the gate. Little Ellen Gillon was amongst this group of children. As Ellen stood in front of the gate, her brother and a few of his friends who were behind it, probably unaware that it wasn't properly attached, pushed the gate and it fell forward on top of the 6-year-old. John Gillon, the little girl's father, a bell hanger who lived at Gladstone Terrace, Bridgend, was walking up the road having just finished work and saw the gate fall on his daughter. He ran to the spot where the accident had happened and lifted the door that was lying on top of Ellen. Blood flowed from her mouth and ears. Mr Gillon carried his daughter to a nearby doctor but she died before any medical assistance could be given.

Sawmill Tragedy

One of the men who worked at Calder, Dickson, Stewart & Company's sawmill in the harbour area of Perth heard a cry of pain from one of his workmates.

HE TURNED to see Robert Mackay holding his side, blood flowing through his fingers. The man leapt over his bench just as Mackay's legs gave way and with a cry of 'Oh Jack', he fell. Luckily, his colleague caught him just in time, and some of his workmates carried him inside. The injured man had been cutting wood with a big steam-driven circular saw when a piece of wood hit the blade and bounced backwards piercing Mackay's side. Although he was taken to hospital, the wound proved fatal and Mackay died on 7 June 1882.

Death in Mill Street

In 1888, the Evening Telegraph reported that on 17 October at the yard of Messrs Wordie & Company, makers of railway carts, the foreman, 61-year-old Duncan McLean, was killed.

HE WAS WORKING in a hayloft above the stables situated in Mill Street, throwing pieces of wood down onto the road below, when he lost his footing and plunged downwards, landing on his head in the street. He died immediately. The paper stated that Duncan had worked for Wordie & Company for thirty years when he was killed.

Young Apprentice Plummets to his Death

In the summer of 1898, work was taking place at the corner of South Street and Scott Street on a large building construction.

ONE OF THE BUILDERS employed in the building works was 13-year-old apprentice lath splitter William Stewart. It seems that when the skeletal structure had been erected, there were no floors in place. Nowadays, it may be inconceivable but one of William's tasks involved walking along the beams in place to bridge the gaps. His employers, Alexander Buist of Perth and Dundee, stated that Stewart was '*very good at walking over joists*'. He had been instructed to carry wood across his body so if he did fall this would prevent his falling through the beams. His employers stated later that he had been told off a few times for failing to comply with this somewhat inadequate and very basic safety precaution.

On 22 August 1898, William Stewart was working at the top of the four-storey building when he fell over sixty feet through the building on to the ground floor. He was severely injured, especially about the head. Three of his workmates took him to the infirmary where he succumbed to his injuries. At an inquiry into the accident (September 1898), Stewart's employers stated that although he had been warned to carry the bars across his body, he was in fact carrying them lengthwise and that was the reason the young lad fell to his death.

* * *

Death at Bridgend

Cattleman George Kidd worked at Muirhall Farm.

ON SUNDAY 5 November 1899, Kidd was taking a cart down what was then known as Asylum Brae and today as Muirhall Road. The road is very steep so 54-year-old George was using all his experience to negotiate the slope. Suddenly, a harness or one of the wooden shafts connecting the cart to the horse gave way, which resulted in Kidd being unable to control the horses; then the cart picked up speed. Kidd struggled to steer the cart and horses as it descended at breakneck speed down to the end of the road. He frantically tried to turn the horses around and follow the road but the horses and cart smashed into the garden wall of *Mayfield House* with a sickening crash. Kidd ended up being thrown into and amongst the thrashing legs of the injured animals. A lamplighter, Peter Chalmers of 10 Tay Street, was a witness to this appalling incident. He ran to the wreckage and, assisted by some other onlookers, pulled Kidd free from the twisted remains of the cart. George Kidd however was dead – the impact with the stone wall had killed him outright.

Death in a Bakery

In the early hours of the morning of Friday 30 January 1903,
38-year-old John McDonald was working in the North Methven
Street premises of the Perth Baking Company.

MCDONALD was working a huge gas powered dough-mixing machine when he lost his balance and toppled in. Before anyone could turn the machine off, McDonald was crushed and died at the scene.

Quarry Tragedy

Patrick Flynn, a 35-year-old quarryman, was killed in Craigie
Quarry in 1904.

HE HAD BEEN using a pickaxe to move loose stone when he hit an old charge of gelignite, which had previously failed to go off and had been forgotten about. When Flynn's pick hit the explosive, it went off and he was killed instantly. At the inquest, Mr McLaren, His Majesty's Inspector of Mines, questioned one of Patrick Flynn's work colleagues about the condition of the old explosives. There seemed to be some disagreement as to

the danger of the shot and how safe it would or wouldn't have been, considering it was a very cold and frosty morning. McLaren seemed to think the frost should have prevented the shot from exploding. The quarryman caused much hilarity in the court when he challenged the mine inspector to prove his theory by placing some explosive on a table and hitting it with a hammer. The mine inspector declined the challenge!

Horror at Jute Mill

It was 14 September 1916 when Peter McGlashan, a 17-year-old apprentice weaver of Castle Gable, walked as normal to work at Crotes Company Ltd, a jute and twine mill.

HE MIGHT have been thinking of seeing his father, for his father had been injured fighting in the Great War. McGlashan Senior had been in an army hospital but was due to be released and would be home the next day. One of Peter's tasks of the day was to assist in the removal of a belt on one of the machines. As the young lad busied himself with the job, someone switched the machine on, with disastrous results. Young Peter's clothes caught on the shaft, he became entangled in the mechanism, and was dragged in. Before his horrified workmates could react, one of his legs was ripped off and he was badly mutilated. Nothing could be done for him and tragically Peter McGlashan was never to see his father again. This was an accident that was not uncommon. In the same mill in 1902, Bridget Mailley was working when she bent down and her hair got caught in a spindle and ripped her scalp off.

RAILWAY ACCIDENTS

The railway seemed to be a particularly dangerous place to work, with newspapers of the time full of accounts of accidents and deaths taking place on the country's rail network.

THE *Edinburgh Courant* newspaper reporting on the death of a pointsman, David Buchanan, in November 1863, stated that his was the fifth fatal accident to have taken place in the last two months. The railway network in and around Perth seems to have been by far the most dangerous place to work in the city.

A man named Robertson, who was a greaser at Perth Railway Station, was found lying dead in a mangled state on the track in 1861.

IT WAS THOUGHT that a passing train must have hit him. On 14 April 1879, a clerk at the station, Alexander Mackenzie, died in Perth Royal Infirmary after having his foot run over by an engine. A wagon inspector, who worked at the station, William Brown, was in 1887 coupling some wagons together when somehow he was run over by three of them and was killed.

When James Reid had some friends from Dundee over to visit him at his home, 43 Kinnoull Causeway, he decided to see them to their train at the station. It was early evening on 27 November 1888 as the group made their way to the station. Reid was a 50-year-old foreman porter at the station, so knew it well. After seeing off his pals, he decided to jump down from the platform and cross the line. As he jumped onto the line, a fellow porter, John Thompson, saw that Reid was in some danger and shouted a warning, which was either ignored or unheard. Reid probably never saw the train that hit him as he crossed the tracks, its wheels sliced through his head just below the eyes and he was killed instantly.

Death of a Guard

On 29 June 1865, a young guard employed by the
Inverness & Perth Railway Company.

JOHN FRASER, was on a train as it entered Perth Railway Station. Life had been good to Fraser: he was a respected member of the rail staff, so much so that he was going to be promoted at the end of the week. This would bring in a little more, much needed, cash for Fraser and his wife as they had only been married for five months. As his train pulled into the station, for some unexplained reason, John jumped from one of the wagons before the train had stopped. As he hit the platform, Fraser lost his balance and staggered backwards. He hit the still moving train behind him and fell onto the tracks. The wheels of the last two wagons rolled over Fraser and he was killed instantly.

Workmen Killed

On 4 July 1884, five surfacemen were busy repairing rails
at Perth Railway Station.

AT THE SAME TIME, an engine was backing into the centre platform to hitch up to wagons full of livestock to go to market. This train normally left from another platform but that one was unavailable so it left from the centre platform instead. Unfortunately, the men working on the line were unaware of this and as the train was backing towards the platform it hit the group of workers, Donald McDonald of Canal Street was cut in two by the train and died immediately. James Bennet of Kinnoull Causeway was also hit and died minutes after the impact. The other three men were fortunate enough to jump out of the way.

A Young Sailor Hit by a Train

John McLellan was a young sailor in the Royal Navy Reserves.

HE WAS with a party of sailors heading south by train in the winter of 1899. When the train stopped in Perth, McLellan and his companions got off the train to stretch their legs and see if some refreshments could be got. For some unknown reason, McLellan walked along the southern end of the platform on his own. When he got to the end, he continued to walk along the tracks. Realising that he was missing, his friends and some railwaymen searched for him. He was found lying by some engine sheds on the side of the track. A passing train had hit him; his arm had been torn off and his thigh was dislocated. It is likely he died from his wounds.

Two Railwaymen Killed

During the afternoon of Tuesday 10 April 1900, between three and four o'clock, a group of men were working on the tracks in one of Perth Railway Station's yards.

AS THE MEN were working, a goods train belonging to the Highland Railway Company arriving from Blair Atholl entered the yard to unload goods. As the train steamed into the yard, it hit the group of workmen, killing John Haggart of Unity Place, a foreman surfaceman who was between sixty and seventy years old and David Craig of 53 Leonard Street who was around fifty to sixty years of age – both were highly experienced railwaymen. The men it seems did not notice the approaching goods train. Both were decapitated on impact; a wagon on the train was derailed. A third man, Mr Balfour, just managed to jump out of the way.

STATION CRASHES

On 28 July 1883, a train travelling overnight from London Euston arrived at Perth Railway Station where it hit the rear end of a train that had just arrived from Edinburgh.

BOTH TRAINS were full of passengers and many of them were hurt by the impact. One man, William Henry Pichens, a footman for the Duke of Sutherland, died from his injuries. At the inquest (January 1884), the engine driver, John Gibson of Motherwell, and the guard, John Johnstone of Bridgend, Glasgow, were charged with culpable homicide and violation of duty. They were accused of approaching the station too fast and ignoring warning signals. Both men were found not guilty, the crash deemed the result of brake failure.

* * *

Lucky Escape for Royal Couple

On 19 September 1899, a train carrying a royal couple stood stationary at the main platform of Perth Station.

THE PASSENGERS, the Prince and Princess of Hohenlohe (a German principality), were on their way to stay with Queen Victoria at Balmoral. It was just after 6am. The princess was still in bed and the prince was sitting in front of his carriage, when there was a screech of brakes and a sickening crash as wood split and splintered and metal twisted and buckled. Wooden splinters and glass flew across the platform injuring several passengers waiting for their trains. The royal carriage shot forward into the one in front. The princess's bed was thrown up onto its end and almost half of the royal carriage was destroyed. After the dust and debris had settled, it became clear that the Glasgow to Aberdeen train had smashed into the royal train. The luggage van at the end of the stationary train took the brunt of the impact and was destroyed; it telescoped into the royal apartments – it was a miracle that the princess was unhurt (she was lifted out of a gaping hole in the carriage). The prince also escaped; and in fact, only a short time later, took pictures of the crash scene with his camera. He was even seen laughing and chatting with the station officials. The passengers on the other two trains were also lucky, no one was seriously hurt.

ACCIDENTS OUTWITH PERTH GENERAL RAILWAY STATION

It was not just in and around Perth Station that fatal railway accidents took place.

Moncrieff Tunnel

On 29 August 1845, during construction of the Moncrieff Tunnel, a workman was killed.

A BUCKET was being lowered down a shaft but it had not been secured properly and slipped off the hook used to lower it. The bucket fell and hit the man below, killing him. The next day, another workman was severely injured by a falling chain but luckily he survived.

* * *

Lost Hat

One Saturday in early October 1854, the mail train
arrived in Perth from London.

AS THE TRAIN stood at the platform, a man's hat was discovered at the very front of the engine. Mr Chalmers, who was the superintendent at the station, organised a search along the line. The body of a man was found in Moncrieff Tunnel lying across the tracks. From his wounds, it was clear that he had been standing on the line facing the train as it hit him. He was later identified as John Davidson, a miller from Logiealmond, who had come to Perth the day before to visit the market. Why he found himself in Moncrieff Tunnel standing facing an oncoming train was never discovered.

OTHER TUNNEL FATALITIES

On 3 March 1873, William Anderson from Blackford was
working at the Moncrieff Tunnel.

HE WAS STANDING talking to a couple of colleagues when a passing train hit his head and he was killed outright. Robert Imrie was working in the tunnel in October 1889, when he was run over by a bogie and killed. Whilst James Callum, assistant superintendent of the railway at Perth, was inspecting the roof of the tunnel in April 1900, he was struck by a train and killed. In July 1903, another railway worker, Robert Ford of Friarton, was working in the tunnel, as a train passed, it caught his trousers and dragged him under the wheels almost severing his leg. In 1910, a plate layer, John McPherson, went into the tunnel to pick up some tools that had been left. He was walking out, carrying the tools and an iron lever slung over his shoulder, when the Glasgow to Perth train shot past. As the train passed McPherson, it caught the lever with such force that John McPherson's neck was broken and he was killed outright.

Never Saw Retirement

John McLaren was an engine driver with the Caledonian
Railway Company.

AS HE LEFT his house at 8 Glover Street on the morning of Tuesday 30 December 1913, he was thinking of the changes soon to come, because at the end of the week he was due to retire after forty-six years of service. McLaren was working on an engine parked just south of the Balhousie signal box, when, for some reason, he left the engine and crossed the tracks. A train, which was shunting wagons into the sidings, hit the old railwayman cutting him in half. Tragically, John McLaren never got to enjoy his retirement.

Twin Railway Tragedies

Sixty-two-year-old Robert Welch had worked as a clerk for the Caledonian Railway Company for twenty-six years.

WHEN HE ARRIVED at his work in Perth Railway Station on the morning of 25 August 1904, instead of going straight into his office, he crossed over to the main platform where he stood and conversed with some friends. Just as the 7.25am train from Edinburgh steamed into the station, Welsh abruptly stopped talking, walked over to the edge of the platform, and jumped in front of the approaching engine. The train had no chance of stopping and passed right over him. When the train had stopped, the horrified onlookers rushed to Welsh's aid. He was lying on the track horribly mutilated, still alive but only just. Welsh died minutes later. The horrific death of Robert Welsh shook all connected with the railway at Perth but more shocking news was in store for them later that day.

A traveller who was journeying to Glasgow was sitting in a compartment on the train with a young woman as the train passed through Moncrieff Tunnel. As the train left the tunnel, the man was surprised to see the woman had vanished. When the train stopped at Forgandenny Station, he expressed his concerns about this missing woman to the stationmaster who got in touch with Perth Railway Station. Immediately, a search party was sent to Moncrieff Tunnel. The party soon found the body of a young woman. She had been run over by a train and cut in two. The unfortunate woman was later identified as Miss Barbara Cowe from Auchterarder. Had she intended to jump from the speeding train to her death or had she fallen by accident? We will never know.

* * *

CHAPTER NINE

The Tolbooth and Other Confinements

THE TOLBOOTH

Unlike today, criminals in the past were not kept in confinement for long periods of time, just long enough for their punishment to be prepared.

THAT IS, unless they were mentally unstable and blameless for their acts of violence, like Patrick Leich. He murdered his wife in 1756 and was sentenced to be confined in the Tolbooth for the rest of his life due to his mental state.

Sometimes, prisoners might be kept in one of the towers of the city walls or in church towers but more commonly those convicted of a crime were incarcerated in Perth's Tolbooth. An ominous building, it sat at the bottom of the High Street where the council buildings stand today. Above the Tolbooth door, carved into the lintel, were the words:

'This house loves peace, hates knaves, crimes punisheth. Preserves the laws and good men honoureth'.

The ground floor of the Tolbooth housed the condemned cell (known as the laigh iron house) for prisoners sentenced to be executed. This cell was twelve feet square and illuminated by a triple iron-grilled window set eight feet from the ground. The door to the cell was made of double oak planks and further protected by a second (iron) door. Inside, the prisoner was chained to the floor. Their bed, a little straw on the cold, damp, stone floor.

Opposite: Perth Prison.

The room above the condemned cell had three iron cages with bars from floor to roof – each cage measured six feet by four feet. Again, the prisoners would be chained to the floor. The next floor up was usually used to house female prisoners; debtors were held in the turrets. A bundle of straw and a blanket would be a prisoner's bedding, fresh water was supplied twice a week, their buckets of filth were removed once a week.

SISTERLY LOVE

Escapes from the Tolbooth were few and far between but did occasionally happen.

IN 1727, Walter Wilson had a visit from his sister. After she had left the Tolbooth, the Keeper of Prisoners in Perth, James Sibbald, noticed some of the inmates whispering amongst themselves. This aroused his suspicions and he entered the cage. Thinking Wilson was lying in his bed, Sibbald went to have a closer look. He pulled back the blanket and was shocked to see that it was not Walter in the bed but his sister. Sibbald was to state, in his defence, that she was the same size as her brother and that they looked very alike. Walter Wilson had swapped clothes with his sister and walked out of the Tolbooth's front door dressed as a woman, right under the noses of the jailers.

MASS ESCAPE

It was a cold winter's evening on 30 January 1838.

AMID A RAGING snowstorm, nine desperate men made a daring mass escape from the Tolbooth of Perth. The men who broke out of jail were a motley crew:

- *Eighteen–year-old James Kerr was charged with murder. From Carron, Kerr has been described as having hard features, a dark complexion, and a stutter. Kerr was wearing a jacket, dark trousers, and a blue bonnet when he escaped.*

- *James Keillor, a thief from Dalkeith, had been convicted of housebreaking in Edinburgh. He was twenty-two years of age and said to be stout with a round face and brown hair. He was wearing a jacket, vest, trousers of white moleskin, and a tartan plaid.*

- *William Boyd from Methven was accused of highway robbery. He had boyish features, perhaps because at the time of his escape, he was only seventeen.*

- *James Morison, a 26-year-old from Falkland had been in prison for theft.*

- *Andrew Hempseed was accused of sheep stealing. He was aged between twenty-five and twenty-eight. (He probably did not know his exact age himself.) Hempseed was described as being slender with a stoop and hard features. It was reported that he was wearing a bottle green short coat, corduroy trousers, and that he usually wore a comforter and sometimes a black silk neckerchief.*

- *Robert McFarlane was a cattle thief apprehended at Doune Market. He was twenty-five or twenty-six years of age.*

- *John Henderson, accused of assault and robbery, was nineteen or twenty years of age with a small thin face.*

- *Peter Morison, a twenty-four or twenty-five year old, was a dance teacher from Kippen charged with assault with intent to ravish. It was said Morison was polite in manner, though his criminal record suggests otherwise.*

- *The final member of the breakout crew was Robert Miller, a 19-year-old thief from Newburgh. He was described as being stout with a round face, a fair complexion, and heavy eyebrows. He was a seaman, which might explain why his hands were said to be black and much chopped.*

The men exploited the renovation work being carried out at the prison. Several iron gates had been removed by workmen, which led the convicts to form a plan. At twenty past seven in the evening, Mr Simpson the jailer and one turnkey (warden) were about to accompany the convicts to their cells for the night. They opened the door of the day room, which contained thirteen prisoners. Usually, one official went into the day room whilst the other stood outside separated by an iron gate but as this was one that had been removed both men had to enter the room containing the prisoners. Suddenly, some of the inmates rushed the two guards and overpowered them. The guards were bound and gagged with napkins and forced into a cell. Their keys were taken and used to unlock the three doors between the desperate men and freedom. The men disappeared into the snow-filled night. Shortly afterwards, the alarm was raised and roadblocks were set up around the city.

On 15 February that same year, a man from Edinburgh was visiting his brother in Auchterarder. As he made his way to his brother's house, he was attacked by three men. They brutally knocked him to the ground and beat him. He was then held whilst he was robbed of all his money and a silver-mounted snuff mill. It was thought that the robbers were three of the escaped fugitives. A reward of ten guineas was offered to anyone who apprehended any of the wanted men.

TAKING THE LAW INTO THEIR OWN HANDS

On one occasion, a prisoner's family could not live with the shame of seeing their loved one hanged publicly in front of the whole city.

IN 1727, three days before she was due to be executed for murdering her own child, Isobel Smith was found dead in her cell shortly after a visit from her parents, brother, and sister. She had almost certainly been poisoned by her family to spare her the shame of a very public death.

Some prisoners did not wait for the law to take its course and took maters into their own hands. In 1752, Francis Hynd was in the condemned cell awaiting execution for housebreaking, assault, and robbery. He was found dead in his cell. He had strangled himself. George Penny tells of one poor wretch who tried to cut his own throat on the morning of his execution but was found before the life had left him. A doctor was called, the man was brought round, and the wound on his neck stitched. He was given enough time to gather his strength after which he was placed on a cart and taken up to the gallows on the Burghmuir to be hanged.

THE FRENCH PRISON

As the wars with Napoleon Bonaparte's France raged, French prisoners-of-war were brought to Britain for incarceration.

IT WAS DECIDED to build a prison to house the French prisoners in Perth. Work began on the prison in 1811. It was constructed on a site where the current prison stands on Edinburgh Road. The cost of the project was £130,000. At the height of the building works, around 1,500 men were employed in the construction. When the prison was opened in 1812, it was big enough to hold up to 7,000 French prisoners in five buildings (130 feet long with outside stairs at both ends). Each of these buildings could hold 1,140 prisoners. In addition to the prison blocks, there were two hospital buildings, a kitchen, a bakehouse, and a washhouse, as well as buildings to hold stores. The entire complex was surrounded by a moat and a wall that stood 12' 6" high. The prisoners were guarded by 300 British soldiers.

First Prisoners Arrive

The first batch of prisoners destined for the new prison at Perth arrived by ship at Dundee on 6 August 1812.

FROM THERE, they were marched to Inchture, where they spent the night in a church, and then they were brought to Perth. It is the duty of captured soldiers to try to escape and attempt to make their way home to rejoin their country's army. Even if this cannot be achieved, at least escaping ties up soldiers and resources involved in the manhunt and recapture of escapees.

* * *

Frenchmen in Perth Jail

*Even as the new prison was being built, the authorities were
involved in hunting down escaped French soldiers.*

ON THE MORNING of 20 April 1811, there were reports that four escaped
French prisoners-of-war were known to be in the area around Perth. A
detachment of troops was sent out to look for them. The fugitives were
captured between Perth and Dundee. The Frenchmen were brought back
to Perth and locked up in the city jail. When one of the jailers opened the
prisoner's cell on the morning of 24 April, he was shocked to find the cell
empty. The prisoners had managed to cut a hole through the wall and
escaped into the courthouse. From there, they dropped from a window
into the street below and escaped. On the table in the cell, the prisoners had
left a letter, where they thanked the magistrates and inhabitants of Perth
for the kindness they received while incarcerated. They promised that
when they got back to France, they would look kindly upon any Scottish
prisoners they might find amongst British POWs.

Successful Getaway

*As the French prisoners settled into life within the new prison,
plans to escape and return home were never far from their minds.*

ON 21 JANUARY 1812, three prisoners managed to escape. They were
helped by a dense fog that had wrapped itself over the land. Hiding and
skulking by day and no doubt travelling by night, the escapees made their way
to Dundee where they stole a sloop (a small sailing boat) and were never seen
again. A woman and two men in the Renfrewshire militia were arrested and
locked up on suspicion of helping the three escapees. (Whether or not the woman
and the two militiamen really did help French prisoners is open to doubt.)

On 8 February 1813, a jailer, as he entered a cell of Perth City Jail, was
hit over the head with a bottle by one of the prisoners. As the jailer lay
stunned, his keys were removed, he was dragged into a cell, and the door
was locked. John Gray, a soldier jailed for desertion, Francis Pirnie,
Alexander Joyce, and Alexander Stewart then made their escape. One of
the Renfrewshire militiamen also in the cell had ample opportunity to
escape too but refused to do so. Perhaps his decision is indicative of his
innocence in the crime of helping the French soldiers escape.

Tried to Bribe Guard

On 22 February 1813, a couple of French prisoners were huddled together with one of the guards speaking in hushed voices.

THE PRISONERS were in the act of bribing the guard into helping them escape and the guard eagerly accepted the Frenchmen's offer of money. But, it was a ruse on the guard's part. Although he offered help, when the conversation was over, the guard went and informed his superiors of the escape plan. The commander instructed the guard to go along with the plan and to turn a blind eye on the night of the planned escape. That night, as the guard played his part, seven prisoners broke out of their block. They hadn't got far when soldiers, who had been lying in wait, pounced on them. The French POWs had been well prepared, as in their possession were scaling ladders, a gold watch, twenty-nine gold coins, and a large sum of banknotes. They were locked in the tower as a punishment.

Tunnel

Just a month after the 22 February 1813 escape attempt, a tunnel was discovered in the WC of Block 3.

IT MEASURED three feet square and its length was forty-two feet, going right under the wall. It seems that the tunnel was discovered just in time, as it was almost finished. Just over a week later, another tunnel was found in Block 2. A prisoner in the prison hospital was suspected of passing on information about the tunnels to the British. When the man was released from the hospital, his fellow countrymen attacked him. It seems they planned to mark him as an informer by cutting off his ears but only succeeded in partially severing one. After being beaten, a rope was placed around his neck and he was dragged to the moat and thrown in. As he struggled in the water, French soldiers jumped on his body with all their force. Things looked very grim for the unfortunate man until a detachment of Durham militia marched into the compound and stopped this attack.

* * *

Cheat a Guard

The French tried again unsuccessfully to bribe a guard into helping them escape, and again the guard informed his commanders.

THIS TIME the prisoners were allowed to get over the wall using a rope ladder they had prepared. Four prisoners were apprehended almost as soon as they got over the wall and another two were found in a ditch. It seems that they had cheated the guard, as the money they paid him was forged.

Three Escape

On 3 June 1813, three prisoners cut through one of the iron bars of their cell window.

USING a rope ladder they got over the wall and made their escape. One man was found hiding in the hold of a neutral ship in Dundee while another was found in Montrose. The fate of the third is unknown, perhaps he made it home.

Bonaparte's Birthday

On 14 August 1812, ten days after the prison had been engaged in the celebration of Napoleon's birthday, a mass escape of prisoners occurred.

THE FRENCH EMPEROR'S birthday had been marked with the launch of a giant hot-air balloon in the colours of the French flag, which was decorated with flags and bunting. This balloon was the work of a French officer from Ghent, M. De Cupyer. Unfortunately for the Frenchman, things did not go according to plan. The balloon was being inflated by burning straw underneath it but it inflated too quickly, was caught by a gust of wind, and broke its mooring ropes. It flew high into the air before returning to the ground and ripping on a tree. A huge crowd on the South Inch who had turned up to see the balloon launch was very disappointed. That night, the whole prison was illuminated to celebrate the French leader's birthday.

As the birthday celebrations were taking place, a tunnel that had been dug from the WC of Block 2 was being completed and on the night of 24 August a large number of French soldiers made their escape. The alarm was raised at 2am when one of the escapees tried to jump the burn that runs along the northern side of the prison and he fell in with a loud splash, which was heard by a guard who fired his musket and raised the alarm. Ten prisoners were captured almost immediately, thirteen remained at large. Several were captured when the high tide prevented them crossing the River Tay. One jumped into the Tay and had to be rescued. Two others, who were hiding on board a boat in the harbour, were caught by the vessel's skipper, and one prisoner was found hiding up a tree.

Four of the escaped prisoners were apprehended in Arbroath on 28 August. They were locked up in the prison there. These prisoners used a piece of iron they had broken from a fire grate to make a hole in the wall of the Arbroath jail but it was noticed before they made the hole big enough to escape from. Three or four of the escaped soldiers were caught and locked up at Forfar and three were taken north of Blair Atholl.

Tunnel Under the Officers' Block

On Saturday 11 September 1813, a tunnel was found in the French officers' block.

IT WAS nineteen feet deep and ran horizontally for thirty feet. As the guards moved into the compound to secure the area while the tunnel was inspected, some prisoners threw stones at the troops. The redcoats responded by firing at the French POWs but nobody was injured. On the Sunday at about 11pm, a sentry noticed about forty prisoners strolling around the exercise yard of Block 3. When they were all herded back into their block and counted, twenty-eight prisoners were missing. The alarm was raised and a manhunt was organised. Two were captured at Bridge of Earn and another two at St Andrews. Three of the escapees stole a sloop in Dundee and a fishing boat was stolen in Kincardineshire. Both boats set sail out into the open sea and presumably onto France.

Two Final Tales and the End of the French Prison

Another two interesting occurrences that took place within the French prison happened in 1813, when two French officers were involved in a duel.

ONE HAD offended the other and both fought with swords until blood was drawn. When one received a wound the other stopped, shook the injured man by the hand, bowed, and apologised.

The other incident took place in the kitchens: a prisoner was employed as a cook in the kitchens when he toppled over and fell into a large pot.

Sadly, he was so badly scalded that he died.

The French POW prison was ordered to close in July 1814 as the Napoleonic wars came to an end. Although Napoleon escaped exile, he returned to France and ultimate defeat at the Battle of Waterloo (18 June 1815).

PERTH GENERAL PRISON

Perth General Prison was built in 1840-1. Prisoners were sent there from all over Scotland.

AT THAT TIME, there were two ways a prison could be run. One was the Silent System in which prisoners would under no circumstances be allowed to talk to one another, the other was the Separate System in which prisoners were kept apart at all times. Perth's prison followed the Separate System. The building must have lots of stories to tell. The following stories have been selected to give a brief insight into the grim existence of the inmates in the prison's early years.

ANGRY YOUNG MAN

In 1853, between April and October, an 18-year-old prisoner was given five days in the punishment cell for destroying a crank machine.

The crank was a device filled with sand with a handle on the outside. Prisoners had to turn the handles of these machines thousands of times a day, giving them time to think about their life of crime as the crank was turned. A screw on the crank could be turned to make the handle stiffer and harder to turn, hence the slang name screws (still) given to prison guards. Days after this young man's release from the punishment cell, he was sent back in for destroying a newly painted wall in his own cell. Again, he wasn't long out when he received fifty-four hours in handcuffs and was put on a third class diet for making a noise, keeping all the other prisoners up all night and smashing a window. Soon after that, he spent three days in the punishment cell for trashing his cell, then another three days for destroying the crank machine again – and yet another three days on the third class diet, this time for throwing a bowl of broth in a warden's face. He might be described as a 'glutton for punishment'.

WOMEN RIOT

A few days before Christmas 1862, 300 female convicts were assembled in the prison chapel.

SUDDENLY, the women prisoners started to cause a disturbance, shouting and wrecking the chapel. When the female wardens tried to put a stop to it, they were attacked. When it became clear that those wardens had lost control, a party of male wardens, armed with pistols were called. They proceeded to fire warning shots over the heads of the rioting prisoners, which had the desired effect of ending the violence. But, there were fears that the men's wings would erupt as several male prisoners had recently been found to have keys to their cells. With the prison on a knife-edge, a powder keg ready to erupt, Perth City Police were called in and soldiers were seen marching through the South Inch towards the prison with fixed bayonets. To the relief of the wardens, things remained quiet throughout the night.

ESCAPE ATTEMPTS

In 1864, two prisoners were being transported south from Perth General Prison to London in a secure railway carriage.

They had somehow got possession of a knife and a shear blade from a pair of scissors. The men managed to hack a hole in the roof of the carriage and climb through it. Despite their legs being shackled, they jumped from the speeding train. One of the men was killed, the other managed to make his escape. He was caught eighteen months later breaking into a house.

A report by the prison manager in 1866 states that there were two ineffectual attempts to escape the prison that year. In the first instance, two male prisoners were caught attempting to saw through their cell bars. A convict who was a known prison breaker made another attempt: he was successful in getting through the ceiling of his cell and then using the ventilation shaft to get onto the prison roof. He made it down into the yard but was captured there.

* * *

ESCAPE ON WAY TO GENERAL PRISON

A young prisoner named Wilson, who was serving ten years, was being escorted from Dumfries to the General Prison in Perth in May 1874.

WILSON had a history of trouble, so the authorities took no chances. Wilson had shackles on his hands and feet, and sitting on either side of him were two prison officials. They were travelling in a third class compartment of a train from Glasgow, which was due to arrive in Perth at 4.20pm. As the train neared Perth, it entered Moncrieff Tunnel, which is 1,220 yards long. In the dark, the guards were aware that Wilson had left his seat and was moving about but it was too dark to make anything out. Presumably, the wardens would have made for the door to the carriage to make sure the prisoner did not try to escape. When the train finally emerged back into daylight, the two prison guards were horrified and stunned to see Wilson had disappeared. They had no idea how he had managed to make his exit, he seemed to have vanished into thin air.

The engine slowed down as it rolled into Perth. As it did, the train driver spotted a figure dressed in white moleskins jump from the train and clamber over a wall that went into an orchard at Craigie. Once in the station, the driver informed the prison guards and the police. Wilson was soon captured by Perth County Police and taken to the General Prison. It is not known just how Wilson managed to make his escape. Did he make his escape while the train was in the tunnel, using the cover of darkness to get out the compartment window, or did he slip out the door before the guards could react and hide out of sight between two carriages before jumping from the train?

ATTEMPT TO SET FIRE TO THE PRISON

In 1880, Henry Bruce was in prison for burglary but was later charged with attempting to burn down the prison by setting alight a quantity of cotton in his cell.

IT IS AMAZING that Bruce was able to do this, as the account of the event details that at the time Bruce was dressed in petticoats and had his hands locked in gloves. The gloves allowed his hands only six inches of movement. Bruce was found guilty and another three months were added to his sentence.

COIN SWALLOWER

Having money while held in Perth General Prison must have made life that little bit easier.

SOME PRISONERS would use desperate and sometimes fatal methods of obtaining or keeping it. Rebecca Bell was sent to Perth General Prison for twelve months for theft in the late 1880s. Shortly after arriving, she started to complain of stomach pains. The pain got worse and worse. She was eventually taken to the infirmary where she died. When the prison doctors investigated, they were surprised to find that Rebecca had swallowed six coins amounting to just over three shillings, which had resulted in her death.

FREEDOM

James Huppell was a notorious housebreaker from Glasgow serving an eighteen-month sentence in Perth when he started to show signs of mental illness and was transferred to what was then known as the lunatic ward.

DURING the early morning of 20 May 1897, Huppell's cell was checked – nothing was amiss. Another check was carried out half an hour later and it was discovered that Huppell had gone. It was easy to spot how he had escaped the confines of his cell, as there was a gaping hole in the ceiling. He had made his way onto the roof of the prison building and from there, managed an eight-foot jump onto the wall. Then he made a fifteen-foot drop into some gardens below and, despite having only one month of his sentence left, he ran for it. It was thought at the time that Huppell found his way to the nearby railway sidings and onto a passing train. He was captured in his home town of Glasgow four days later.

* * *

CABBAGE PATCH KILLING

Joseph Thomson was clearly a troubled man.

FOR SOME TIME, friends had been getting strange letters from Thomson. His own mother received a letter in which he referred to a violent fantasy he had regarding his wife:

'In the cupboard in the front bedroom lies a dagger ready for its final plunge home. But I must have her [his wife] down first if it be the will that she go'.

Perhaps his friends and mother were not that surprised when, at his house in 3 Langside Place, Glasgow on the night/early morning of 15/16 March 1927, Thomson beat his wife to death with a hammer, cut her throat, and stabbed her with a dagger. It was clear at his trial that he was not in a fit mental state to plead, so he was locked up in the lunatic ward of Perth General Prison indefinitely.

In January, he had an altercation with another inmate, 31-year-old Patrick Drummond from Lasswade in Midlothian. On 25 July 1928, both men were working in the prison garden, along with fourteen other inmates. Two wardens were in charge, one patrolling the wall and the other in the tool shed. Thomson, who was described as 'a dour, sulky man, who kept himself to himself and never mixed',was forking a cabbage patch. He made his way to the toolshed and asked the warden for a spade to trim the edge of the cabbage patch. Spade in hand, Thomson walked towards Patrick Drummond, who was described as an 'inoffensive little chap'. Thompson lifted up the spade and brought it crashing down on Drummond's head.

Warden Edward Falconer was patrolling the wall when he heard a shout from one of the prisoners. He looked over just in time to see Thomson smash the spade down on Drummond's head. Falconer blew his whistle. Thomson who was readying himself to hit Joseph again, dropped the spade and walked towards the warden with a pale look and staring eyes uttering the words:

'It's over now. I have done him in'.

Drummond was taken to the hospital but died from his injuries. At an inquest, it was decided that there was nothing that could have been done to prevent the tragedy.

AN OPPORTUNITY 'TWO' GOOD TO MISS

On Thursday 25 September 1924, a group of prisoners were working, harvesting vegetables in a field adjoining Perth General Prison.

THE ONLY THING separating the men from freedom was a spiked iron fence topped with barbed wire. Despite a prisoner escaping a month previously, the warden in charge pushed a wheelbarrow loaded with produce in through the main gate, leaving the prisoners unsupervised. This was too good an opportunity for two of the inmates who soon absconded, getting over the perimeter fence without difficulty. When the alarm was raised, the authorities acted quickly and it was clear these men could not have travelled far. Both were picked up in an orchard near Aberdalgie that evening.

UNABLE TO CONTAIN THE PRISONERS

Three prisoners made a daring escape on 7 August 1925, while working in a vegetable field within Perth General Prison.

SIX MONTHS EARLIER, two convicts were recaptured near Amulree in the Sma' Glen after they too had escaped. As with the previous escape of 1924, the vegetable field was walled by a spiked iron fence topped with razor wire. The latter batch of escapees were Alex Bickerstaff, William McKee, and Alex Chalmers. In common with the previous escapes, all the men were prisoners incarcerated in the prison's mental hospital. The prisoners simply used a ladder that had been removed from the prison store to climb over the fence and into an adjacent woodyard belonging to James Jones & Sons Ltd. The police, who must have been well used to searching for escaped convicts in and around Perth, acted quickly. Work-yards, gardens, and sheds in the immediate neighbourhood were all searched, road blocks were placed on the major routes out of the city, and the railway sidings that run close to Perth General Prison received special attention. Alex Chalmers was the first to be captured. He was apprehended in the nearby woods.

In Auchterarder, a policeman, Sergeant McIntosh, who had just been informed of the escape, noticed a lorry going through the town; unusually there were two passengers sat by the driver. Suspicion aroused, McIntosh followed the lorry on his bike through the town. He stopped the vehicle. Inside the cab sat child murderer Alex Bickerstaff. Incredibly, Sergeant McIntosh got on a service bus to Perth with the prisoner and after a pleasant journey through the villages of Forteviot and Dunning, dropped the prisoner off outside the prison gates.

Only William McKee remained at large. He made his way to Dundee where busking on the streets with a rendition of the song *Danny Boy* soon earned him enough money to purchase a change of trousers and boots. Unfortunately for McKee, he was spotted acting suspiciously in Dundee Railway Station by Mr Watt, an ex-policeman, who apprehended him despite being warned by McKee:

'I've done better men than you'.

In the end though, he gave up without a struggle.

The newspapers made a big play about the fact that during a period of eighteen months, nine prisoners had managed to escape from Perth General Prison. It must have been a frightening time for the people who lived in and around Perth with frequent alarm signals warning them that dangerous and desperate convicts were on the run.

EVADING CAPTURE

At 6.25am on 26 November 1928, as Perth was waking from its slumber, Robert Paterson, alias James Wilson, escaped from his cell within the confines of Perth General Prison.

HE USED a piece of wood with nails hammered into it at intervals to make a rudimentary ladder and made his way over the prison wall. It was a full two hours before the wardens noticed he was missing and a search was launched. Paterson, from Kinross, was a thief who was serving a six-month sentence for robbing the Forgandenny post office, a shop in Methven, and a garage in Dollar. He knew the area well having worked in farms around Forteviot and Forgandenny. So, he decided to make his way back there. Despite a large manhunt, no trace of the escaped convict could be found until late afternoon, when the gamekeeper of the Moncreiffe Estate spotted a man wearing prison clothes hiding amongst the young trees. Sixteen police officers and six wardens were drafted into the area but despite this the prisoner escaped. He remained on the run for two months, until some locals informed the police that despite it being winter, a man was sleeping rough, begging for food and seeking farm work. Sergeant Reid of Perth County Police made his way to the area, disguised as a farmer riding a motorcycle. Reid soon observed a scruffy man walking across a field towards the village of Saline. The policeman left his motorbike at the side of the field and pretended to be inspecting the animals. He was soon approached by the man who struck up a conversation and asked if he had any farm work. The policeman led the man on for a bit until he was sure the man was the escaped convict and arrested him.

In a further twist to this story, Paterson was released on 28 March 1929. The big heavy prison gate had just slammed shut behind him and he had barely taken in a lungful of air as a free man when Sergeant Reid approached him along with an Inspector Davidson and rearrested him on further burglary charges.

SUCCESSFUL ESCAPE?

This is a remarkable story involving the supposed escape of a prisoner from Perth.

ON 8 AUGUST 1933, the police were carrying out searches in Bridge of Earn and Abernethy for Mary Rooney McConnachie, a 28-year-old Ayrshire woman who had just escaped from Perth General Prison. What is amazing about Mary's escape is that it happened in broad daylight. She was cleaning the officers' quarters and jumped out of an unbarred window before calmly walking out of the prison without being recognised, despite wearing her prison uniform of dark gray shirt and skirt with black stockings. A person bearing her description was seen getting into a fairground show lorry and it was thought she was on the road to St Andrews. As time went by and no trace of the escaped convict could be found, questions were being asked.

When a prisoner in Perth General Prison was found to be missing, a bell was rung in the prison. But when Mary escaped this was not done and no discarded prison issue clothing had been found. Then the mystery deepened with the supposed recapture of Mary Rooney. Although the Perth City Police and the County Police had been heavily involved in the search for this woman, neither party were informed of where she was found. There seemed to be a great deal of secrecy and mystery involved in her apprehension. As the officials and press demanded an explanation, gradually the story became clearer. It seemed Mary had not escaped the confines of the prison after all but had instead managed to hide within the prison for a week, much to the embarrassment of the prison authorities.

PRISON GOVERNOR'S WORST NIGHTMARE

A concert had just finished in Perth General Prison on the evening of 13 October 1938.

THE PRISONERS' otherwise mundane lives had been somewhat enhanced by a group of vocalists who performed for them that night. As the prisoners were led out the room, shuffling past the performers, Helen Heggie, a well-known vocalist who lived in Scott Street, suddenly gave a terrifying scream and fell to the ground. Amidst the confusion, it soon became apparent that something awful had just happened, an event that would surpass the worst nightmares of the prison authorities. For sticking out of Miss Heggie's back was the wooden handle of a makeshift knife (fashioned from the metal hoop of a barrel with a wooden handle tied with string). One of the convicts had quite deliberately plunged it into her. Other prisoners standing near the attacker grappled with him and by the time the guards took charge, he had been knocked unconscious. He was taken and locked in his cell. As the poor woman lay on the floor, one of her party tried to pull out the knife but the handle came away in his hand leaving the blade embedded in the singer's back. Heggie was taken to the infirmary and underwent an operation to remove the weapon. Her attacker was 37-year-old George Yuille from Glasgow. Heggie was awarded £162 in compensation for the attack. As for her assailant, he died a few months later of natural causes.

* * *

THIS·HOUSE·LOVES·PEACE·HATES·KNAVES·CRIMES·PUNISHETH
PRESERVES·THE·LAWS·AND·GOOD·MEN·HONOURETH

CHAPTER TEN

Crime Does Not Pay

CRIME IN THE DARK

Perth, like any other city, has had and has its fair share of crime.

IN THE PAST, matters were not helped by the poor street lighting that gave would-be robbers the perfect cover. Smash and grab raids on shops, for example, were once a common occurrence.

Gangs armed with small lead coshes tied to their wrists would roam the streets after dark. These gangs would lie in wait, ready to pounce on anyone merrily making their way home from the city's drinking establishments unaccompanied. Young boys who sold pies around the various inns and taverns would act as paid informants to the gangs. They would tell them who was in the tavern, how much they were drinking, and when they were getting ready to leave, making them suitable prey for the robber gangs. Thankfully, improved street lighting was introduced in 1782, making the streets of Perth much safer.

ESCAPING JUSTICE

At the circuit court, a man was brought before the judge for theft.

HIS EYES were rolling around in his head and he started to throw bits of bread at the startled judge, raving about how the bread would protect him

---

Opposite: "This house..." plaque (Council Building, Tay Street).

from witchcraft. The court ruled that the man was clearly insane and the case was dismissed. The same man returned to the court a while later for stealing cattle. Again, he acted very strangely. The jailer from the Tolbooth, where the man had been held, was called. The jailer stated that the man was heard telling a fellow convict that he was not worried about his case as he was sure he would fool the judge like the last time. The jailer said he was sure that this man was *'more rogue than fool'*. The man was found guilty and sentenced to be transported. It is claimed that the thief escaped before the sentence could be carried out.

HIGH JINKS

A young lad was brought before a Perth councillor, Bailie Allison.

THE BOY'S CRIME was climbing up the steeple of a church to ring the bells. This, it seemed, was a common and dangerous dare that the young boys of the city often perpetrated – much to the annoyance of the citizens and the authorities. Allison decided to make an example of the boy and gave him a two-month prison sentence. Before this was done, the lad asked if he could say something in his defence. This was granted. The boy stated that he was not the only one climbing up to ring the bell that night. When asked to name the other youths, the boy named Allison's son as being there. The bailie thought about matters before deciding to reduce the sentence to a warning.

BAILIE EMBARRASSED

One of the magistrates in Perth was Bailie Duncan, better known as Jamaica Pete.

HE LIKED a good drink and was very fond of the lassies and often kept company not befitting his title and position. He had a habit of drinking in notorious drinking dens, one of them a bakery owned by Robbie Aiken. Among Duncan's drinking buddies was Perry Mitchell, a notorious rogue. One night, Mitchell was drinking in a dodgy den when a fight broke out. One of the chief instigators of this fracas was Perry Mitchell. The authorities were called and many were arrested but Mitchell escaped. He was picked

up shortly afterwards and taken to court to be charged. Bailie Duncan was the judge that day. When he asked Mitchell if he had been involved in the fight, Mitchell claimed that he wasn't even there that night. He stated in front of the whole courtroom to a mortified Duncan that the last time he was at that particular establishment, he was drinking with the bailie himself! He went on to say that the bailie should remember the night because someone knocked on the door, causing Duncan to take fright and hide in the oven. Mitchell finished off his scandalous speech by declaring that when they got the all clear, the bailie came out and they both drank together for the rest of the night.

* * *

DIVINE INTERVENTION*

> *Sometimes people seem to get away with murder but then over*
> *time, fate can become judge, jury, and executioner.*

IN ONE SUCH CASE, a young lad who lived in the Watergate and came from a respectable family, fell foul of the law. His sentence was to be whipped through the city. His mother frantically pleaded for mercy on her son's behalf but the sentencing bailie was having none of it – the sentence would be carried out. As the young boy was being led through the Watergate, his mother once again begged the bailie to release her son from the ordeal. When the bailie refused, she fell to her knees and cried out a curse on the bailie's children – that none of them would ever live to the age of her son and, if they did, she hoped that they would be made to suffer as her son suffered. It was noted that none of the bailie's children lived to be older than the woman's son.

During the Jacobite rising of 1745-6, Scotland was in turmoil as war gripped the land. An English traveller rode into Perth and took lodgings with a family in South Street. It was noted how carefully the man looked after a large case he was carrying. The man then seemed to vanish, neither he, his horse, nor the case were ever seen again. With the war raging, no one had much time to properly investigate the man's disappearance. But what was noted amongst the people of Perth, was the fact that the family who the Englishman lodged with seemed to have come upon a windfall – they were splashing the cash. Suspicions grew but there was no proof of any wrongdoing, even though the locals remarked that since the Englishman was lost, every child born to families living in South Street was born insane and that it was God's judgment. When the house was pulled down in 1808, the truth was revealed: a human skeleton was found buried under the hearthstone in the kitchen.

In 1777, Bailie Henry Fife's (or Fyffe) young son obtained a commission in the army, becoming Lieutenant John Fife. Whilst on leave, he came to Perth. He was out drinking one night when he had an argument with James Taylor, a flax dresser from the Skinnergate. The bailie's son drew his pistol, shot, and killed Taylor. For this, John Fife was arrested and held in the Tolbooth. He was tried for the crime but pleaded insanity. When he was found guilty, he was sentenced to be locked up for life. Fife's father pulled some strings and after paying £100 security, the young soldier was transferred to serve his sentence at home in his family's house. This angered the public as Bailie Fife was unpopular and deemed to be a harsh man who showed little sympathy when sentencing offenders. Fate however played its own hand. The bailie's luck changed, his business failed, and he died a poor man.

A farmer named Robertson was last seen drinking in a house in Kirk Close, belonging to James Ross, a brewer. The farmer had just come into a large amount of money through selling his goods at market. When the farmer failed to return home, his family became extremely worried, so they contacted the authorities in Perth. A search was made for him and James Ross was questioned. Ross claimed the missing man had left his premises alive and well. Eventually the farmer's body was pulled from the River Tay. From the state of the corpse, it was clear it had not been in the river long and drowning was not the cause of death. Suspicion fell on Ross and although nothing could be proved, people shunned his business, which suffered as a result. He became poor and desperate. Eventually, Ross tried to drown himself in the Tay but was saved. Madness gripped him and he lost his mind along with all his possessions. Ross spent the rest of his life in a straitjacket, tied down to a bed. When he was visited by a local minister, Ross appeared to want to confess to something but his wife was nearby and sensing that her husband might say something that would see them all hanged, she stepped in and quietened him before ushering the minister out. Ross was not the only household member to be afflicted in some way. His sister-in-law, who lived with him, became paralysed down one side of her body.

A publican in the Speygate had a vicious argument with his wife as she cradled their baby in her arms. The publican lashed out violently, the blow missed the woman but struck the child, killing it. The man fled Perth, trying to evade justice by going overseas. He boarded a ship and appeared to have escaped justice. During the voyage, the ship was caught in a storm, and was lost along with all its passengers and crew.

---

* If the above stories are true, it seems fate was busy at one time in the city of Perth, dishing out its own form of justice.

* * *

CHAPTER ELEVEN

Punishment

HUMILIATION, MUTILATION, AND EXECUTION

At one time in Scotland, there were three main methods used
to punish wrongdoers: humiliation, mutilation, and execution.

HUMILIATION

The punishment of humiliation was exactly as it might be
thought to be. The culprits would be put in a position where
their peers could ridicule them publicly.

A Wolf Tamed

The most important man publicly humiliated in Perth was
Alexander Stewart, Earl of Buchan, Earl of Ross, Lord of Badenoch.
STEWART was the third surviving son of King Robert II, grandson of
Robert the Bruce. Stewart was also known as the Wolf of Badenoch, for
despite being the son of the king, he led a band of outlaws that terrorised the
north of Scotland. It was his dispute with the Church for which Stewart is
most remembered.

Although he was married to the Countess of Ross, Stewart sought
recognition of, and perhaps even permission to marry his mistress Mariota
Athyn. The Church would not sanction Stewart's wish and the Bishop of
Moray, who in a dispute had lost lands to Stewart, had him excommunicated.

Opposite: Mercat Cross symbol (High Street).

The Wolf of Badenoch retaliated by riding with his men to the town of Forres in May 1390 and destroying the church buildings there. He then made his way to Elgin where he burned down the cathedral, known then as the Lantern of the North.

For his crimes against the Church, Stewart was ordered to Perth to publicly repent and make peace with the Church. He was forced to come to Perth Castle and there in front of a vast crowd, which had come from far and wide to see that proud arrogant man humbled, was made to walk barefoot, wearing sackcloth, to the church of the Blackfriary. There he knelt before the Bishop of St Andrews and publicly repented and asked for forgiveness for his actions.

A Royal Curse

In 1627, the wife of John Keir, who had assaulted her husband with a pair of fire-tongs, was sentenced to walk through the streets of Perth on market day, barefoot and holding the tongs above her head.

IN 1752, Thomas Low and Thomas McManus were drinking in one of Perth's taverns when both were heard to curse George II and drink the health of Bonnie Prince Charlie. For this, they were both made to walk from the Tolbooth to the Highgate Port with a sign on their breasts that read in large letters:

'*For Cursing the King*'.

They were also banished from Perth for three years.

MUTILATION

The second form, or level, of punishment was mutilation.

THIS REQUIRED a criminal to be physically marked as such, either by branding or by the slitting of an ear or nose. In the case of a thief, a whipping of the back would be followed by the branding on the body of a letter '*T*' (for thief).

In 1737, Margaret Smith (or Smyth) was found guilty of pickery (pick pocketing) and of being in the burgh whilst under a previous order of banishment. For this crime, she was whipped on her naked back around the city by the common hangman. She was then put into the Tolbooth for several days whereafter she was released and whipped again. Finally, Smith was put in a set of jougs (an iron collar) with one of her ears nailed to the Tron (Perth's public weighing machine used to weigh goods sold at market) and burned on the face with a branding iron before being banished with a warning that if she ever returned her punishment would be more severe.

EXECUTION

The ultimate punishment was death.

MOST sentences of death involved hanging but drowning and being burned at the stake were also methods of execution used in Perth. The places of execution in Perth were the Mercat Cross; the Burghmuir, which overlooked one of the main roads into the city; the North and South Inches; the square behind the Court House; and Perth General Prison.

THE MERCAT (MARKET) CROSS

If you were found guilty of committing a crime and you were sentenced to be punished in Perth, you would normally be taken to the Mercat Cross.

THIS STOOD at the eastern end of the High Street. Today, all that remains of the Mercat Cross is an octagonal figure marked into the pedestrianised High Street (opposite the entrance to the Skinnergate). The date the first market cross was erected in Perth is unknown. The second was built during the reign of James VI on the same site. It had a balcony surrounded by steps and a cellar underneath. City officials would gather on the balcony during important anniversaries such as the monarch's birthday when they would publicly drink to the monarch's health. Public proclamations and announcements were made from the Mercat Cross and the names of wanted criminals would be attached to the cross. The busy market would operate around the Mercat Cross, the beating heart of the city.

The original market cross of Perth was pulled down in 1651 by Cromwellian troops and the stone used in the building of a citadel on the South Inch, as detailed in chapter two. For the following eighteen years, Perth had no cross, until a new one was erected in 1669. Owing to the increased amount of horse-drawn traffic in the High Street, the Mercat Cross was moved to its present location in King Edward Street in 1765.

As previously mentioned, the site of the cross was used to administer minor punishments but hangings were also carried out at the cross. In 1707, John Blair, who had been found guilty of committing adultery, was sentenced to stand at the Mercat Cross with a written declaration on his breast:

'This is one adulterer with Helen McQuhattie'.

Blair was then stripped to the waist and whipped through the city by the hangman. In a wee side note to the story, ten years later in 1717, a warrant was issued for the execution of Helen McQuhattie for murdering her own child.

THE PILLORY

Adjacent to the Mercat Cross, stood a pillory.

THIS wooden structure had a large hole for a criminal's neck and two smaller holes for his/her wrists. It should not be confused with stocks, which held a criminal only by the legs and/or wrists. The pillory stood in the centre of the High Street surrounded by a flight of steps. Criminals would be forced to stand there in all weathers for however long the court decreed. People would come along to mock and hurl things at them. Rotten fruit and vegetables, dung, dead rats and cats, and basically anything disgusting lying around the market could be used as a projectile – especially if the offender was not well liked or the populace frowned upon their crime.

In 1587, the Kirk Session decreed that anyone in the city caught fighting, scolding, nagging, or committing slander shall be apprehended by the city bailies and be put in the pillory for ten hours. They were also to wear the branks, a device that fastened around the head with an iron bar, which was inserted into the mouth to sit on top of the tongue and stop the wearer from talking. After this, they were ordered to pay a fine to the poor and on the following Sunday to go to church where, for the entire service that sometimes lasted hours and hours, to sit on the stool of repentance in front of the whole congregation. When the service was completed, they were required to get down on their knees and beg forgiveness from the people affected by their crime.

On one occasion the city executioner, Sandy Dow, had to place his own daughter in the pillory. No doubt this was done in front of a large crowd, all mocking and cheering him, full of self-satisfied glee. Dow speaking to the very amused mob said that his daughter had brought shame on him and he was *'clean affronted with her'*.

The quiet peace on the Sunday night of 12 June 1620 was shattered as the Common Bell was rung. This startled the citizens, as it would usually signify some sort of alarm. It turned out that the city was neither on fire nor under attack.

Rather, Alexander Wilson who had had quite a night, decided to ring the bell. Earlier that day, Wilson met Giles Lowry, who had just returned from escorting her friend home, and placed the woman in a state of fear. He then went on to terrify another woman before grappling with the servant of Matthew Chap in the Kirkyard. When a man intervened and came to the aid of the scared woman, Wilson ran into the church and proceeded to ring the Common Bell. For this, he was placed in the pillory for three hours.

In 1699, Ewen Cameron, a notorious common thief, was sentenced to be taken to the cockstool. The term cockstool is suggestive of a stool or seat used in a similar manner to a pillory – to publicly humiliate. There, Cameron had the lap of his right ear cut off by the hangman before being banished from Perth.

Robert Laing was placed on the pillory for one hour in 1740 for stealing a comb and some garters from James McLaren, a chapman (travelling salesman). Laing was also banished from Perth. Charles McLean, a journeyman coppersmith, stole from his master and was fixed to the pillory for one hour then banished from the Burgh in 1751. The punishment of the pillory was handed out regardless of gender. Anne Napier who stole cloth from a bleachfield in 1775, was sentenced to stand on the pillory bareheaded, with a piece of cloth about her shoulders and a sign affixed to her:

'Theft from a bleachfield'.

The pillory was still in use in Perth at the end of the 1700s. In 1795, James Rob was placed on the pillory for one hour with a sign around his neck:

'Infamous Forger'.

He was subsequently banished from Scotland for seven years.

* * *

WHIPPING

One punishment commonly used in Perth, was to be publicly whipped by the hangman.

THIS WOULD often be done at the Mercat Cross but sometimes the offender might be scourged (whipped) through the city. When this happened, the culprit was stripped to the waist, tied to a cart, and a procession travailed through the city led by the city drummer.

The route usually began at the Mercat Cross, then headed down the Watergate, up South Street, and back on to the High Street by way of Meal Vennel. At each point, the cart stopped and the lash was administered. On one occasion in the 1700s, a riot broke out, after five people, who had been part of a mob, were to be whipped through the streets of Perth. The three men and two women had been protesting about food shortages in Kirriemuir.

Realising that there was a great deal of sympathy for the culprits and a real potential for trouble, a party of dragoons were called out. On the morning the sentence was due to be carried out, the dragoons were stationed at the jail door to provide the authorities with an armed escort. As the prisoners were brought out, the mob pelted the troops with stones. The procession got under way, entered the Watergate where again the troops came under attack. Maintaining discipline, the soldiers escorted the prisoners and city officials into the wider expanse of South Street. There, the crowd had grown in size and the violence escalated. Stones and rocks rained down on the official party; three of the soldiers were dragged from their horses and severely beaten. In Meal Vennel, things quietened down due to the street being narrow but when the punishment party emerged into the High Street, widespread fighting between the mob and the soldiers broke out and the dragoons' rearguard was completely cut off from the rest of the group. The remaining dragoons turned their horses around and with drawn swords charged up the street. The crowd took to their heels, running for their lives away from the galloping horses' hooves and the slashing swords. Those who could not escape on foot threw themselves into shop doorways or down closes. It was a miracle no one was killed.

In 1699, Andrew Craigdillie was scourged through the streets for theft. In the same year, four men were forced to stand with one ear nailed to the gallows before they were whipped through the city. Each had a piece of one ear cut off – all were banished. Another man was whipped below the gallows before being branded upon the brow by a red-hot iron. In 1701, Grisall Robertson, whose crime was reset (receiving stolen goods) and theft, was whipped through Perth. Her right ear was nailed to the Tron, and after that her ear was slit. In 1714, at the three most public places in Perth, the hangman whipped George Baxter and Marion Anderson, then nailed an ear of each to the Tron. Again, they had the lap of their ears cut off before being set free. In 1732, Janet Stewart, Isobel Ross, and Marion Crocket were whipped through the streets before being ejected from the burgh. They were vagrants or unlicensed beggars. Two women were found guilty of reset of stolen cloth in 1735. They were whipped each Friday until they were banished.

Perhaps the saddest story regarding public whipping in Perth took place in 1739. Three boys, William Bissat, Thomas Taylor, and David Millar, had been caught stealing linen yarn from the weavers. As the three boys were underage they were not to be whipped by the hangman but by their own fathers and in the presence of the city magistrates, who were there to make sure the sentence was carried out correctly. After the whipping, the boys were banished for a while – a sentence every bit as hard for the fathers as it was for the youngsters.

Perry Mitchell, who appears in the tale of the *Perth Bailie Embarrassed* was a notorious character. On one occasion, he was arrested and held in the Tolbooth. The provost was told about the arrest of this habitual criminal and made an off-the-cuff remark that Mitchell deserved a good whipping. With this remark still ringing in his ears, a city official made his way to the Tolbooth and told the jailer that the provost had ordered Perry Mitchell to be whipped. The hangman was sent for and Mitchell was stripped and led out into the street. A large and curious crowd had gathered. The provost looking out of his window saw the throng of people and asked what was happening. You can imagine his panic when he was told Perry Mitchell was to be whipped. Running on to the street, the provost only just managed to stop the punishment being carried out without the proper sanction of the court.

* * *

FORNICATORS

At one time sex before marriage was a serious crime,punishable by death and it was up to the Court or Kirk Session to punish those suspected.

DAVID GRAY was a violent man, who beat his wife when she accused him of seeing another man's wife. In August 1584, he thrashed Helen Watson until she was black and blue for rejecting his sexual advances. Helen must have succumbed to his charms for in the same year both she and Gray were hanged at the Market Cross for committing adultery. It is said the execution was carried out opposite Watson's mother's yett (front gate).

William Young lived alone, so his housekeeper, Violet Paterson, who made his meals, would often eat with him. This was enough to arouse the suspicion of the ever-vigilant Church and in 1580 the pair were ordered to appear before the Kirk Session. William was told that he must publicly repent in the Kirk and stop seeing his housekeeper both publicly and privately. Violet did not accept this decision so easily and she violently protested her innocence. This is understandable as her employer could simply employ another housekeeper but she had lost her job and with her reputation in tatters, getting another would be very difficult. Such were Paterson's protests and open defiance of the ministers and church elders, she was banished from the burgh. In 1585, James Pitlaidy, a barber surgeon, was told he would be paid forty shillings a year to shave the heads of those found guilty of fornication. When Thomas Smith confessed to fornicating with three different women, he was sentenced by the Kirk Session to be held in the Tolbooth, to have his head shaved, and then ducked in the river. He fled the city but after he and anyone caught sheltering him was threatened with excommunication, he submitted himself to the Kirk. One of Thomas Smith's conquests was a woman called Barbra Brown. After making her repentance publicly, Brown sought out the company of Thomas Smith. For that, she was made to stand at the Mercat Cross locked in irons on market day. She was also told to stay away from Smith unless he married her. In 1585, Janet Will had her sentence of having her head shaven and being ducked suspended until after she had given birth to the baby she was carrying.

In 1588, the midwives of Perth were made to promise under oath by the Church that they would never come to the aid of any woman giving birth who was suspected of being an adulterer. This law also required midwives to inform church elders if they were asked to deliver a child when the mother had not disclosed the name of the baby's father. This shameful act was reaffirmed in 1593.

As John Gibson lay on his deathbed surrounded by ministers and church elders (in 1593), he felt the need to get something off his chest. In confessing to fornication, Gibson betrayed Elspeth Culross who was forced to make her public repentance before the congregation at church. In 1602, Janet Sym and John Barrie were locked up at their own expense before being paraded together around the city in a cart. They were then both banished.

LYING WITH SOLDIERS

The military had an active presence in Perth and many soldiers, whilst on leave with money to burn, found Perth's fair maids irresistible.

MARY GORDON, who, described as *'an idle vagrant'* was banished for one year for whoring with soldiers. There is a fantastic note by Major James Wolfe (of Culloden and the capture of Quebec fame) to the provost of Perth regarding Mary Gordon. Wolfe offered to put into the Provosts hands *'one of the most wicked and abandoned harlots ever tormented a regiment of foot'*.

In 1751, Agnes Graham was banished for lewdness with soldiers and poxing several of the regiment garrisoned in Perth. Elspeth Ferguson was banished for a year in 1752 for cohabiting with soldiers. Christian Robertson, who was the wife of the city hangman Patrick Grant, was banished for six months for lying carnally with two soldiers in 1753; and Jean McLean, another married woman, was banished in 1755 for consorting with soldiers. Anne Peddie and Janet Gould were arrested in 1778 for being in a *'disorderly house'* in the city with soldiers and were given the choice of going into service or leaving the burgh.

* * *

BANISHMENT

Being banished from Perth was a common form of
punishment, as some earlier stories evidence.

THE CRIMINAL would be taken to the city gate, forced to bend over, and the hangman would ceremoniously kick them up the bum. This was to indicate the city's disdain at the individual and show that the city did not want the person back for either a set period of time or in some cases for life. Banishment was a bit of a problem if your home, family, and work were all within the Burgh of Perth. If you were marked by a branding iron before being banished it was even more of a problem, as you would not be let into other towns or cities.

In 1587, the Kirk Session found David Innes guilty of being a filthy speaker. For blasphemy, David was banished from Perth for life. Janet Robertson, from Alyth, was caught stealing at a fair in Perth in 1724. She was scourged by the common hangman, sent over the water (the Tay), and told never to return to Perth. In the same year, Catherine Firskin stole a candlestick, snuffer, and snuff dish from the Dower Duchess of Atholl -for this crime, she was whipped and banished.

The following year, Janet Gorie and Jean Donaldson were found guilty of reset of stolen cloth and they were whipped each Friday until being banished. John Malloch was found guilty of theft and resisting arrest. For this, his whole family were banished. In 1750, Agnes Brown was banished for a year for stealing two napkins from Margaret Robertson. The desperation felt by Helen Stewart, a vagrant, can still be felt, even after so much time. Her husband was in the Tolbooth waiting to be punished and she was desperate. She was banished in 1752 for giving ill language to the provost and for threatening to bring her hungry children and leave them at the provost's door.

Criminals banished for a set time who returned early could expect to be treated very harshly if caught reoffending. In 1744, Jean Dougal was banished but she returned too soon and was caught stealing the following year. That time, her sentence was to be committed to the public workhouse for six months before being banished again. Grizell Bayn was banished for unlawfully living with soldiers. She too returned prematurely and was put into the workhouse for three months before she was banished once more.

SLAVERY

In December 1701, four prisoners who lay in Perth Tolbooth under sentence of death had their sentence changed by the commissioners to perpetual servitude, a state amounting to being someone's property, a slave.

ONE OF THE MEN, Donald Mcdonald, was gifted as a perpetual servant to the Earl of Tullibardine. It is recorded that McDonald had to wear around his neck a collar of brass, iron, or copper with the inscription:

'Donald McDonald, found guilty of death for theft at Perth, December 5th 1701, and gifted as a perpetual servant to John, Earl of Tullibardine'.

If McDonald attempted to escape, evading capture would be very difficult with the collar, and capture would mean the original sentence of death would be carried out.

TRANSPORTATION

With the discovery of the New World, the authorities started to transport criminals to British-held territories overseas.

TRANSPORTATION could be for a few years or for life and sometimes the prisoners would be forced to work on plantations as virtual slaves. Theodore Lyon, a thief, was banished in 1784 for life and was to be sent to His Majesty's plantations in America. Theodore somewhat optimistically sent a letter to Mr Millar, Perth council's clerk, asking to be transported somewhere with a warm climate. He suggested Grenada where he claimed he had a friend who would take him!

Banishment was administered for what today seem like minor crimes. In 1800, James Hall and James Walker were transported for five years, after being whipped for stealing two pieces of cloth; and in 1817, John Dykes was banished overseas for seven years for stealing some silver spoons from the house of Ann Cameron.

The saddest case of punishment in Perth must surely be that of the two prisoners who in 1813 were sent to the transportation hulk *The Retribution*, which sat on the River Thames at Woolwich. The two, David Ritchie a ditcher and Alexander Laing a private in the 92nd Regiment of Foot, were thieves. Both felons were 7-year-old boys. The fear they must have felt locked in the hold on board the overcrowded and disease-ridden *Retribution* surrounded by hardened criminals is almost unimaginable.

* * *

THE MONCRIEFFE ARMS

CHAPTER TWELVE

Killing in Perth

INFANTICIDE

The killing of a child is a repulsive crime that goes against the natural instinct to protect and nurture.

IT IS PARTICULARLY hideous when the killer is the child's mother. In the days before birth control when society very much looked down upon unmarried mothers, poverty and the lack of a welfare state meant that some mothers had heartbreaking decisions forced upon them.

In 1589, the Church convicted Nicola Brown (of Perth) of killing her child through neglect. Her punishment was to turn up at church the following Sunday dressed in sackcloth and be placed upon the stool of repentance, which is surprisingly lenient.

Elizabeth Robertson was hanged for killing her own child in 1721. Margaret Craig and Janet Black were also hanged for infanticide in 1730 and 1734 respectively.

Not Abandoned Prostitutes

Agnes McDongall was sentenced to death for murdering her child in 1751 but this was changed to transportation to the colonies.

IN 1762, a death warrant was issued for Mary Burges, a servant to John Sprunt of Airntully, a hamlet a few miles north of Perth. At the time, Mary

Opposite: The Moncrieffe Arms.

was being held in the Tolbooth of Edinburgh, as she had been found guilty of murdering her own child. A warrant was issued to transport her to the Tolbooth of Perth to be hanged on a gibbet. Her body was then to be handed over to a Perth surgeon, Neil Menzies, for public dissection. It is doubtful that Mary Burgess suffered this fate, as there is no record of the implementation of her death penalty in *The Encyclopaedia of Scottish Executions*. It is more likely Burgess had her sentence commuted to a more lenient penalty. Evidence for this is found in an article published in the *Scots Magazine* in 1762, the same year Burgess was imprisoned. The article considers the cases of a number of women found guilty in the Scottish courts of killing their own children. Importantly, the article acknowledges that many women who kill their children are '*not abandoned prostitutes, but generally, young women unhappily seduced, or perhaps actually ravished'*. The author states that these woman have '*a strong sense of shame'* and a '*well-grounded dread of great contempt and pinching poverty'*. The article also claimed:

> '*A method could be fallen on to transfer a just share of the shame to the other sex, when their folly has such a tragical issue; that as a woman is punished capitally if her child be found dead, because she has not previously taken the proper methods for its preservation, she suffers, not for committing a crime, but for neglecting to do her duty; that surly nature never meant to burden the weaker parent with the whole care of the offspring in any stage of its infancy'*.

The article can be interpreted as a clear sign that attitudes regarding the punishment of women who murdered their children were starting to change in the mid-seventeenth century. This changing thought process on infanticide did not however save Jean Cameron who was a servant to an excise officer in Dundee. She had had a relationship with a soldier and fell pregnant. The fear of losing her job lead her to conceal her pregnancy and kill her newborn baby. For this act, she was hanged in Perth on 19 October 1764. Jean Cameron was the last woman to be hanged in Perth.

* * *

Tossed into the River Tay

In the early hours of the morning of 28 June 1876, some fishermen were hauling in their nets from the River Tay below Perth.

AMONGST the catch lay the tiny body of a baby. The child had not been in the water for very long. The infant was well dressed, wearing a white satin hood, white flannel square, white pinafore, black and mauve checked frock, a black and gray striped petticoat, white flannel petticoat, white flannel barrie, and white stockings. From her clothing, it was obvious that the young girl had been well looked after.

The police took the body to the police station. They were not sure if the child had been deliberately thrown into the river or if perhaps it had been a tragic accident and both mother and child had fallen into the Tay. Would another body be found? These questions remained unanswered until a woman walked into the station and told the police that she had heard an argument in a house in South Street the night before. The row seemed to be all about the cost of keeping an illegitimate child.

Officers made their way to the premises on South Street where they spoke to a 23-year-old mill worker, Jessie Alexander. Alexander was apprehended on suspicion of murder. At her trial in October 1876, Alexander explained that after a quarrel with her mother about the maintenance for her child, she had been thrown out of the house. She took 5-month-old Isabella Gordon to a spot where the River Tay runs along the northern edge of the South Inch and tossed the youngster into the water. The court found Alexander guilty of culpable homicide and sentenced her to eighteen months' imprisonment.

Killing in the Moncrieff Arms

Margaret Guthrie Gentry, a 38-year-old cook, worked in the Moncrieff Arms in 1888.

SHE WAS desperately trying to conceal the fact that she was carrying a child. On 24 April 1888, she complained to her employers that she was unwell and left the premises. Shortly after her fellow servants noticed some things, which made them think that perhaps Gentry had just given birth. A Dr Simpson was called and a search was carried out. In a room, behind a fire grate, the tiny body of a baby boy was found. The doctor concluded that the child had died as a result of being suffocated. Gentry was arrested and tried. The charge of killing her child was not proven but she was found guilty of concealment of pregnancy and given nine months' imprisonment.

Deadly Fathers

Pierce Hoskins had been a soldier serving in America and the East Indies.

HE MAY have been suffering from what at one time was described as shell shock and now as post-traumatic stress disorder. Whatever mental disorder he suffered from, whether it was a result of his experiences while serving in the army, it was certainly made much worse by alcohol. On 17 September 1811, Hoskins '*flipped*' with violent and deadly consequences. Several witnesses saw his frenzied knife attack on his 4-year-old son. When he was tried in April 1812, it emerged that Pierce was overtaken by a temporary fit of insanity. He was ordered to be locked up indefinitely.

Suffocation in the High Street

Duncan Clark was charged that on 22 October 1825 he committed infanticide:

'*In the High Street of Perth, and near the town-clerks's office of Perth, wickedly, barbarously a feloniously place a living female child, which had recently been born, the daughter of Christian Cameron, then and now or lately residing in Earlsdykes, situated in the East Church parish of Perth and which had been delivered into his custody, as the father, or the alleged father, of the said child into an escritoire or writing desk belonging to him, in his house aforesaid; and he did shut, or forcibly press down the lid of the said escritoire or writing desk up-on the said child, and did lock the same, whereby the said child was compressed and suffocated to death*'.

WAS THIS some sort of terrible accident or a cold-hearted murder?

Whatever had happened to the infant girl in Clark's home, the fact is, she was a shock and surprise to this middle-class professional man. His daughter had been born to Christian Cameron, a poor Gaelic-speaking girl who lived at Earls Dykes at the western edge of Perth. A witness at the trial,

Ann Cameron, stated that the child was born at the end of harvest or beginning of winter. She also told the court that she was not at the birth but arrived a little while later. The child was given a little punch for sustenance, dressed in a flannel petticoat, a printed frock and a barrie, and handed by the mother to Ann Cameron, Isabel Cameron, and Margaret McNab, the baby's half-sister. The women were instructed by the mother to take the child and give it to the father. When the women arrived at the home of Duncan Clark, it was a shock to say the least. He told them to take the child back to her mother but they refused, telling him to find a nurse. Clark left to go and obtain the services of a nurse but returned saying that he could not find one. He asked Mary Robertson if she could look after the child until 7pm, telling her he was looking after it as a favour to a gentleman and was taking it to Bridge of Earn that night. Mary refused to babysit the child. It became clear that the women were not going to leave until he had found someone to look after the child, so he left again, returning a short while later saying he had found a nurse and she would be round in half an hour. The women left but only went as far as the home of a Mr McLeod who lived at the foot of the stairs. They saw no sign of a nurse but did witness Clark come and go several times on his own without the child.

Worried for the child's welfare, the women obtained the assistance of a man called Halley and a town-officer, David Garrick. They went up to Clark's home where there was no sign of the baby. Clark told them that he had sent the little girl to a nurse in Bridgend. Halley and the town-officer went to Bridgend in search of the baby but on failing to find any sign, returned to Clark's house.

There was still no sign of the baby, who hadn't been seen since the three women had handed her over to Clark. Ann Cameron, Isabel Cameron, and Margaret McNab were adamant the child had not left Clark's house but Clark insisted he had taken the baby to Bridgend. He reluctantly agreed to accompany Garrick and Halley to Bridgend, where they went to a pub called *Jackson's* and Clark left the two men to fetch the nurse and child. Clark returned stating the nurse was afraid of the town-officer so had refused to come. As the three men left *Jackson's*, Halley turned to Garrick and stated, '*this is all a joke, for there is no child belonging to him there at all*'. Both men took Clark to see Mr Duncan at the Fiscal's Office where Clark maintained the child was safe and in Bridgend.

The sheriff ordered a search of Clark's house but nothing was found. Duncan was kept in custody as he could or would not give a satisfactory account regarding the whereabouts of his baby daughter. Another search of the property was carried out on 24 October. It was only then that the police noticed a locked writing desk. They called for George Garvie, a blacksmith, who picked the lock. Inside the desk was the dead body of the missing baby.

As his trial, the prosecution had to prove that the child had been deliberately killed and had not died as a result of an accident or by being neglected while Clark was leading everyone a merry dance as to the child's whereabouts.

A number of witnesses were called. Things at the trial were complicated when Ann Cameron was asked to repeat the oath and remained silent. Like the rest of the women, Ann could not speak any English. Luckily General Stewart of Garth was on hand to translate for the women. Dr Malcom, who was called to Clark's house after the body of the baby was discovered, stated that in his opinion the child had been dead when it was placed in the writing desk. Another physician, Dr Stewart, agreed with Dr Malcom's evidence. Then Dr Johnston from Dundee stated that though he agreed the child had been put into the desk while dead, there was no sign of violence and without dissecting the body, it was impossible to say for sure how the child had been killed. Dr Christison, a professor of medicine in Edinburgh stated that the child might have died of natural causes and then been placed in the writing desk.

There seems to be some contradiction from the medical experts as to the child's death: was it a crime or simply a tragic accident?

After hearing all the evidence, the jury retired only to return after a quarter of an hour to declare the prisoner guilty with a recommendation for mercy. The judge, Lord Gillies, sentenced Clark to be executed on Friday 3 November – his body to be handed over to the surgeons for dissection. On hearing the sentence read out Clark collapsed and had to be helped out the courtroom.

That is not the end of the story. George IV on the advice of the Prime Minister changed the death sentence to that of transportation for life.

Clark was never transported. He died in appalling conditions in the bowels of an overcrowded, filthy, and disease-ridden transportation hulk.

Deadly Stepfather

Robert Ford Duff was a young man of twenty-three years when he married and took on the role of stepfather to his wife's young 4-year-old daughter, Margaret Dougal.

BY ALL ACCOUNTS this young glass-tube maker was good with children; singing funny songs to his sister's children. The family were settled in the Craigie area of Perth.

Being responsible for someone else's child can be a thankless task, especially when the step-parent first comes into the child's life. They can resent the new relationship with their parent and make things difficult. Perhaps that is what Robert was experiencing with his new young charge but that could never excuse his actions. Shortly after the marriage, Duff began being violent towards the young girl, a violence that escalated to such an extent that he killed her on 28 January 1910.

For this truly awful crime, he was sentenced to death. Two days before the sentence was due to be carried out, Duff was given a reprieve and transported from Perth to Peterhead Prison, where he would serve his life sentence. However, by September of that year, he was removed to Murthly Asylum.

MURDER

Battered Old Woman

On 9 February 1850, Catherine Ferguson inflicted a prolonged and violent attack on Janet Farquharson of Thimble Row, an old woman of sixty-eight years whom she had been nursing.

CATHERINE had been looking after the woman when for some reason she *'lost it'*. She leapt on the bed with Janet and sat on her, pressing her weight on her chest, while beating her with her fists and twisting and crushing her fingers. Janet suffered fractured ribs, a broken arm, and several fingers on both her hands were broken. She died on 22 February. Catherine Ferguson pled guilty to murder but was given just eighteen months' imprisonment.

* * *

Murder, Murder?

*As the town of Perth was awakening from its slumber early
one morning in May 1861, a woman threw open her window
in South Street and was heard to scream 'murder, murder' at
the top of her voice.*

A COUPLE of brave souls shot into the close and up the stairs two at a time
while someone else ran to find a policeman. All must have wondered just
what hellish events were being carried out above. As help arrived, the
woman threw open her door and cried that there was a *'black man'* in her
house who had come to cut her throat. She was shaking and hysterical and
quite clearly very scared. When the room where the supposed attack had
taken place was entered, the man turned out to be the local chimney sweep
who had been working on the roof and somehow had toppled down the
woman's chimney.

It is easy to picture this poor woman being woken by a crash, opening
the door to the room from which the noise emanated, and on seeing the
chimney sweep covered in soot and presumably shaken and swearing
loudly, she panicked and mistook the chimney sweep for someone who had
broken into her house with evil intent. Luckily, neither the woman nor
sweep suffered any lasting injuries.

Murder or Tragic Accident?

*One cold February night in 1864 (the 18th of the month),
Walter Macdonald, a tobacconist who lived in Charlotte Street,
was woken by his wife.*

THE COUPLE listened as an argument raged outside. Loud voices could be
heard and a couple of minutes later a splash. It sounded like something had
been thrown into the Lade. Two stories above Macdonald's home, a
window opened and Helen Clark, a servant to the property owner, a Mr
Scott, looked out. She too had been woken by the noise and had heard the
sound of something or somebody entering the water, although all now
seemed quiet down below.

The next morning, Sergeant John McGillvery of the Perth police
spotted a woman lying face down in the Lade behind Charlotte Street. She
was lying with her head upstream and her arms above her, obviously dead.

She was taken to the town's Dead House and identified as 57-year-old Margaret Forbes, wife of Duncan Forbes. A quantity of money was found on the body: 2½d in a purse and 16s 7d in a pocket sewn into her skirt. Her husband told the police that his wife had earned some money by selling three pigs to a flesher called Mr Fenton in the days leading to her death.

During the investigation, Forbes told the police that on the night of her demise, Margaret had left the house at around 7pm. She had been drinking and would not tell her husband where she was going. Shortly after she left her house, she was seen drinking in a grocery shop in South Street. Peter Lynch, the proprietor, told the police that Margaret was in the company of Cornelius Kelly who had at one time lodged with Margaret and her husband. Margaret seemed to be supplying Kelly with drink, as he had admitted to a labourer called Kennedy who was drinking with them that he had no money. According to Kennedy, Kelly said that he hoped he would have some money later that night.

By 10pm, Forbes and Kelly were drinking in the *Camperdown Tavern* in town with Robert Robertson, a cobbler. Robertson stated that Margaret was paying for the drink. He thought she had about £1 in silver and a £1 note, which she kept in a handkerchief. As he was leaving, he warned Margaret to '*take care of her Siller*' [silver]. (During the investigation, Robertson was apprehended in connection with Margaret's death but later released.) Christina Strachan, the daughter of the owner of the *Camperdown Tavern*, told the police that when Margaret and Kelly left at about 11.20pm, she thought the woman was staggering. She also stated Margaret had £2 in silver, which she took from a white cloth.

The intoxicated couple made their way to the *Strathtay Tavern*. William Shaw the innkeeper gave them a drink but when asked for a room for the night, he refused. Margaret left the tavern followed shortly by Kelly. Shaw was to state that as he left, he heard Kelly shout '*where are you?*'. He then heard footsteps in the close, going, not out to the street but the other way, towards the Lade. Shaw then retired to bed. Ten minutes later, he heard heavy footsteps walking quickly away.

Cornelius Kelly was arrested and charged with murder and theft. At his trial in May 1864, he pleaded not guilty. Statements were read from several witnesses and the prosecution argued that Kelly's motive seemed to be getting his hands on Margaret Forbes' money (the full amount was never recovered). The turning point in the trial came when two doctors both agreed that they would have expected to see signs of violence on Margaret's body but there were no signs of an attack and struggle. They concluded that death was by drowning. Margaret's liver indicated she was a heavy drinker, so she might have simply fallen into the Lade while drunk. The jury agreed and found the case against Cornelius Kelly not proven and he was allowed to walk free.

Did Margaret Forbes in her drunken state slip and fall into the Lade on the night of 18 February 1864? Or, did her death have a more sinister explanation? Whether it was murder or a tragic accident, we will never know. The only person with the answer was Cornelius Kelly.

Drunken Fall?

Charles Scott, a tanner of about sixty years of age, lived with his wife, son, and his two grandchildren (a boy and a girl) in the Kirkgate. Scott and his wife were known to like a good drink.

ON THE NIGHT of 7 April 1866, passers-by heard a terrible argument between the drunken couple. The following morning, Mrs Scott was found dead. Her husband was arrested but during his trial not one medical expert could safely say that the woman's death had been caused by an act of violence carried out by her husband. It could just as easily have been as a result of a drunken fall. The verdict was not proven and Scott was released.

On the night of Mrs Scott's death, her son, a rope spinner, was taken home drunk by two policemen. Mrs Scott was also intoxicated – she was put to bed by two women who told her to be careful not to fall out of bed. On the night she died, her son in a drunken stupor fell out of his bed and suffered a cut to his head. As for the cry of murder, a report of the case in the *Dundee Advertiser* of 21 September 1866 explained that Mrs Scott was often heard shouting murder for no apparent reason even when she was alone. The report claimed that when sober Charles Scott was good to his wife and gave her his wage packet at the end of the week. The not proven verdict was in this case probably the right outcome.

* * *

Death in the Kirkside

Thomas Gibbons lived with his wife Rose in Kirk Close
by the Kirkside.

THEIRS was a turbulent marriage – his wife had thrown bowls and coal at him in the past. On the night of 19 April 1868, the couple were rowing again. The neighbours heard someone cry *'murder'* and *'police'*. Later, Gibbons walked into the police office and told the night inspector that his wife was *'either dead or dying'* as she had fallen backwards whilst attempting to sit down on a stool. He was immediately arrested and two police officers made their way to the Gibbons' home where they found Mrs Gibbons dead. Despite maintaining his innocence at his trial in July 1868, Gibbons was found guilty by a majority of ten to five and sentenced to three months' imprisonment.

Unfit For Publication

When Mrs Margaret McKenzie made her way to Perth's poorhouse,
it was clear that she was in need of urgent medical attention.

BLEEDING HEAVILY from a terrible internal wound, she was put in the infirmary. Nothing could be done for the poor woman as her insides and genitals were badly mutilated. As she lay dying, she confessed that her husband James McKenzie, a hawker, had deliberately carried out these injuries to her insides during a violent sexual attack at their lodging house in South Street and she had lain for three days, bleeding heavily before seeking help. James was arrested for what was by all accounts a sickening crime. The newspapers of the day were horrified and declared the details unfit for publication.

Margaret McKenzie never recovered. She died in the infirmary of the poorhouse on Friday 11 January 1889. With the death of the only witness, the charges against her husband were dropped.

Attempted Murder and Suicide in the High Street

The police were called to the address of James Christie in the
High Street, in early November 1893.

WHEN THEY forced their way into the house, they found the body of David Young, the Christies' lodger. He was lying in a pool of blood on the floor with his throat cut. In another room, the police found Christie's wife and her friend Jane Sime. They had both been very badly beaten about the head and face with a hatchet, which lay nearby. The two women were still alive and were taken to the infirmary for treatment. It seemed that Young had argued with the two women and, in a fit of rage, attacked them both with the hatchet. Leaving them badly injured, he then went into the other room and, perhaps through remorse for his actions, slashed his own throat.

Wife Murderer

At 7pm on the evening of 16 May 1905, Mrs Jane Murray, who was regarded as hard working and industrious, returned from work.
AS SHE CLIMBED the stairs to her home at 23 Guard Vennel, she was tired and hungry. Murray had stated earlier to colleagues that she was going to get some supper, as she had not eaten all day.

Guard Vennel was full of housing inhabited by the poorer citizens of Perth. Most of its family homes were single-room rented accommodation. Mrs Murray and her Irish husband, James, had lived at the property for about two months. James Murray, a 45-year-old labourer, had come to Perth to work on the erection of the new tramlines that crisscrossed the city. When that project was completed, the Murrays stayed on in Perth.

James Murray liked a drink and on the night of the 16th, he had had a skinful. By about 9pm, he was loudly rowing with his wife. It was so loud that a neighbour of the Murrays, a Mrs Pringle, went up and knocked on the Murrays' door. James Murray opened the door and threatened to give Mrs Pringle the same as his wife was getting. Next, a Mrs Birrell went to complain about the noise; Murray answered the door and kicked her down the stairs. Mrs Pringle opened her window and called to two policemen who were passing. The two officers went up to speak to Mr and Mrs Murray. This had the desired effect for a while but the rowing started again a short time later.

About midnight, James Murray staggered down the stairs, clearly intoxicated. He met two neighbours, Robert McKean, a carter, and William Burrell, a labourer. He told them '*there was something far wrong with his wife*'. The police were called and when they entered the house they were met with a sickening sight: the floor was soaked in blood. The poor light, offered by a flickering paraffin lamp that sat on the mantelpiece of the room, revealed Mrs Murray lying on the bed, wearing only her stockings. Blood pooled on the floor and had soaked through the floor onto the ceiling of the house below. Mrs Murray's battered body was bruised all over and her scalp had been almost ripped completely off of her head. Mr Murray sat on the edge of the bed wearing only a pair of trousers. James Murray was charged with murder. Still suffering the effects of drink, he seemed almost unaware of what was going on.

At a packed courtroom on 26 June 1905, James Murray was found guilty of culpable homicide and sentenced to seven years imprisonment. Despite being such a rough area in the city, full of the most desperate and poorest, this was the first murder in the Guard Vennel since John Martin beat Alexander Gray to death there on 1 January 1895.

Horror on South Street

William Mitchell, a 57-year-year old blacksmith, sat in his house in Cow Vennel. Living with him were his partner, Mrs Campbell and her 21-year-old daughter, Mary Ann Campbell.

JUST AFTER 8pm on 16 April 1914, Mitchell sent Mrs Campbell Senior out to get beer.

When the older woman was away shopping for Mitchell, Mary Ann who had been at the public washing house washing some clothes, came home to the two-room house. Just what was said between the two in the house remains a mystery. Passers-by in South Street were startled by a loud cry of '*murder*' before seeing Mary Ann run out into the street covered in blood. She was in a hysterical state and near collapse due to the amount of blood she had lost. She told the startled passers-by that William Mitchell had attacked her with a knife in her home as she sat drinking a cup of tea. The girl had deep defensive wounds on her arms, hands, face, and wrists. She had managed to fight him off and flee the home, first going to the house in the Cow Vennel opposite and getting a drink of water from Mr Angus who lived there, before staggering dazed, weak, and blooded into South Street.

The police were called and when they went into the premises it was clear that a violent struggle had taken place in the kitchen: there was blood everywhere, smashed crockery, and upturned furniture. The police followed a trail of blood into the next room. William Mitchell lay slumped on his knees beside a chair, around him a large pool of blood. One hand hung limply at his side, in the other the razor that he had used to cut his own throat from ear to ear.

Cutlass Killing

Charles Lamb was a 62-year-old painter who lived in Canal Crescent with Williamina Mowatt Young and her sister, 28-year-old Christina.

LAMB did not like the fact Christina maintained a friendship with a married man, William Brough Bannerman, who would visit the home in Canal Crescent at the end of each week. During these visits, while Christina and her sister chatted away, Lamb would sit quietly brooding away, clearly disapproving of the relationship and openly hostile to Bannerman.

The relationship between Bannerman, a former boxer who liked a drink, and Christina was seemingly platonic. She believed that by inviting Bannerman to her house it would keep him from frequenting the local pubs. But it was clear Lamb thought there was more to the relationship than mere friendship. Bannerman had remarked that he might shake the old man up sometime to teach him a lesson.

On the night of Sunday 24 March 1929, Christina was walking home from church when she met Bannerman in South Methven Street. She was to say later in court that Bannerman was quite sober and accompanied her to her house. Lamb had been in and out of the house but returned around 10pm and went into his room. At 10.15pm, Christina told Bannerman it was time he was going home. She walked him down the stairs and on to the street. As the couple said their goodbyes, Lamb looking out his window was heard to remark *'get to your bed you dirty devil'.* A red mist descended before Bannerman's eyes and the blood rushed to his head. He turned around and ran up the stairs. When he burst into the house, he was confronted with Lamb holding a cutlass in one hand (with the blade pointing towards the ceiling) and its sheath in the other. Unperturbed and still raging, Bannerman grabbed Lamb's wrists and the two men grappled in the middle of the room. Christina, who had run up the stairs behind Bannerman, put herself in between the two men and almost immediately cried out '*Oh it has cut me*', having suffered a cut to her hand. This served to inflame Bannerman's passion. As the fight reached the fireplace, Bannerman attempted to pull the cutlass out of Lamb's hand. In this act, Bannerman was cut deeply at the top of his thigh and began bleeding profusely. Exclaiming '*I am wounded, send for a doctor*', he staggered into the kitchen and collapsed on the floor. Nothing could be done to help as the life drained from the big, powerfully-built, former boxer.

At his trial in July 1929, it was decided that as Lamb had been attacked by a much younger, stronger, and fitter man, and had not pointed the blade of the weapon at his attacker (he had kept it pointing upwards until Bannerman had grappled with him), he had not meant to kill. Charles Lamb was found not guilty of culpable homicide.

Shooting on Buckie Braes

This is an incredible case, with many twists and turns and is likely to be one of the most incredible murders ever to have taken place in Perth.

ON 14 August 1935, a young engaged couple were out walking on Buckie Braes, which lies to the west of Perth, just a stone's-throw from the Glasgow Road. The couple were Daniel Kerrigan, an 18-year-old apprentice glazier and keen junior footballer, and his young fiancée, 17-year-old Marjory Fenwick. The couple were walking and chatting, perhaps planning their future as Mr & Mrs Kerrigan, when suddenly from the bushes out stepped a man carrying a shotgun. He fired at Kerrigan hitting him on the face, neck, and chest. Kerrigan fell to the ground mortally wounded. The attacker then rifled through the injured man's pockets and took out a pocket book and a wallet. He grabbed Fenwick by the hair, dragged her from the path, and brutally sexually assaulted her.

The crime shocked the whole town and a massive manhunt was launched for the gunman. The search for clues was not helped when a fire broke out on Buckie Braes, a fire that could destroy vital evidence. '*Was this fire started deliberately by the killer?*' people asked. Then, stranger still, the dead man's sweetheart and the only witness to the slaying received a sinister and threatening letter, claiming to be from the killer. The letter had a Dundee postmark and ordered her to come to the Dundee platform of

Perth Railway Station on the following Saturday at 6.30pm to meet a *'Man in Blue'*. After the story had been released to the local press, that Saturday there was the comical spectacle of vast crowds gathering at the train station, all looking for the strange man in blue. Needless to say, he never turned up. Two men, one wearing a blue suit, were seen on Buckie Braes on the day of the shooting. Perhaps the blue-suited man was the mysterious letter writer.

The Perth police were struggling with the case, so on the same day that Fenwick received the letter, two of Glasgow's finest detectives arrived in Perth to give assistance. A local man out walking found a pair of hidden green gloves but they did not belong to Fenwick. Some passengers in a train leaving Perth spotted a gun lying near the tracks. This was picked up by the police but was found to be a German army rifle dating from 1916 and unconnected with the murder.

Later, a man went into a pawnshop in Dundee and tried to sell a shotgun. When the pawnbroker informed him of the illegality of firearms trading, the man left. This sparked a manhunt in Dundee and eventually the man was traced. He still had the gun in his possession but the police were satisfied with his story that the gun had been in a gunsmiths undergoing repairs for the last five weeks and so could not be the murder weapon. When a man seen acting suspiciously in Canal Street was arrested late on the night of 18 August, hundreds of citizens, many wearing their nightclothes under their jackets, came out into the street. The man however was released without charge and allowed to take the late bus home to Auchterarder. Fever gripped the city.

During the attack on Fenwick, the assailant had tied her wrists with a handkerchief. It was discovered that the handkerchief was stolen from the laundry at Aberdalgie House, along with a telescope and a purse. The police questioned a farm labourer, 24-year-old John M'Guigan, about being in possession of a shotgun around the time of the shooting. When he could not account for the weapon, as it was no longer in his possession, he was arrested.

M'Guigan was tried at the High Court in Edinburgh. Fingerprints linked him to the break-in at Aberdalgie House and witnesses on Buckie Braes gave evidence that they had spotted him on the day of the attack.

One even claimed to have seen him spying on couples with a telescope. Upon his arrest, a handkerchief was found in his jacket pocket, which matched the one tied around Fenwick's wrist. Also found in his possession was Fenwick's suspender belt. Despite all this evidence, M'Guigan pled not guilty.

It took the jury just over two hours to come to a verdict. They stated that M'Guigan was guilty of breaking into Aberdalgie House Laundry and stealing the handkerchief, telescope, and purse. He was also found guilty of raping Fenwick but incredibly, on the charge of the murder of Daniel Kerrigan, the verdict reached was not proven.

M'Guigan was sentenced to ten years for the theft and attack on Marjory Fenwick but no one was ever charged with the killing of the young man.

Something out of a Horror Film

Just how long 40-year-old Duncan Doig, reportedly belonging to the town of Crieff, sat brooding in his lodging house at Carlile Place is not known.

HIS MIND was filled with deep and deadly thoughts for inflicting a terrible revenge on the woman who had in his troubled mind, wronged him. He left Perth to get some work labouring in the countryside but his mind still buzzed with dark thoughts of a bloody reckoning.

On the night of 4 May 1942, Elizabeth Ryan who stayed in a house in Ruthven Avenue on the Crieff Road went to bed. Also staying in the building was her 20-year-old daughter Annie Macnamare, who was often known as Nancy Ryan. Elizabeth's daughter had only being staying with her mother for a few months after coming over to Perth from her native Ireland. When Nancy came to live with her mother, Duncan Doig also stayed at the house. Perhaps Nancy had persuaded her mother that Doig was no good for her or maybe mother and daughter needed more space but whatever the reason, Duncan Doig signed over the tenancy to Elizabeth and left the property soon after Nancy moved in, a very angry man.

At around 3am, Doig walked towards the Ryan home, trying his best to conceal the shotgun he was carrying. He had borrowed it from a friend saying he needed it to shoot pigeons. Ryan sat bolt upright in bed, listening as the sound of glass shattering violated the stillness of the night. Terror must have gripped her very soul when she realised someone was climbing into the house through the bathroom window. This noisy forced entry must have woken Nancy because she made her way to her mother's room. Did Doig taunt the women trapped in the darkness, telling them what he had planned for them and why they were going to die? We may never know.

What we do know is that Ryan and Macnamare made a frantic last ditch attempt to flee by smashing the bedroom window. Before they could escape, the neighbourhood was woken by two loud bangs, followed a short time later by another one.

When the police entered the house, they found the bodies of mother and daughter dead in a bedroom, and Doig lying barely alive with terrible injuries to his face and head. He was taken to the infirmary but died a short time later.

* * *

CHAPTER THIRTEEN

Execution

DROWNING

Drowning was a method of execution normally reserved for females as it was believed to be less cruel than hanging!

WHAT WE would regard as really minor crimes today were punished in a drastic and cruel way in the past. In 1522 or 1523, Margaret Lockhart was drowned in the river for stealing a silver belt and a pot.

In 1543, during the religious unrest of the early days of the Reformation, James Ronald, William Anderson, and James Finlayson fixed a ram's head and a cow's tail to an image of St Francis. They also hung a noose around its neck. This was after an altercation in the church when Robert Lamb who, influenced by new religious thought and practices coming from the continent, considered the old Catholic religion as outdated and corrupt, got involved in an argument with a friar. Helen Stark, Lamb's wife, was also in trouble with the authorities for refusing to pray to the Virgin Mary during childbirth, saying she would pray to God instead.

With all this unrest, the Catholic Church decided to take action and make an example that the people of Perth would not forget. Ronald, Anderson, Finlayson, and the Lambs were sentenced to die along with James Hunter, a simple soul seemingly found guilty by association. The men were to hang and Helen Stark was to be drowned. She asked if she

Opposite: Strathallan Castle.

might be allowed to hang alongside her husband but the request was refused. The condemned prisoners were locked in the Spey Tower whilst the preparations for their executions took place. On the day of the executions, Stark was allowed to accompany her husband to the gallows. There she watched him and his fellow religious reformers die. She was taken to a pool of the River Tay, her suckling infant was taken from her breast, and she was drowned.

HANGED IN PERTH

Many criminals would have been hanged in Perth over the centuries. A lot of the records of these executions have been lost. This chapter nonetheless hosts a selection of culprits who ended their lives on the end of a noose in the Fair City.

The Last Jig

For the vast majority of criminals sentenced to death in Perth, the end came whilst doing a macabre dance of death at the end of a noose on the gallows.

AS DETAILED EARLIER, the main sites for execution in the town were at the foot of the High Street near the Market Cross and high up on the Burghmuir overlooking one of the main routes into Perth.

At the gallows, the prisoner would be made to climb up a ladder that rested against the gibbet. The noose would be placed around his neck and when the signal was given, the condemned would be pushed off the ladder into oblivion. Later, a scaffold with trapdoor was constructed in front of the centre window of the council buildings at the foot of the High Street. A wooden beam, with noose attached, projected out from the window and the same proportion of beam projected inside the building. Under the room a weigh-house was constructed. Here, a rope with a heavy weight fastened three feet from the floor was secured to the beam in the room above. When the condemned was placed in the noose, the weight in the weigh-house descended causing the beam outside to lift and the criminal would be hanged.

*   *   *

The Common Hangman

The town hangman, often referred to as the common hangman,
had an important job to do.

HE LIVED in a house in Mill Street, which was supplied by the council. The hangman was eligible to take one piece of coal from every load that was brought into the town. In those days, coal came in big lumps that you would have to break yourself. The hangman could also claim one fish from every fishing boat that unloaded its catch in the harbour. Most towns would also let the hangman have a cup of meal from every sack that was brought into the town. The hangman was paid a flat rate, with a bonus every time he punished or executed someone. He could work in other towns that did not have a hangman where he would receive payment plus travelling expenses. After an execution had taken place, the hangman could keep the clothing of the criminal. He would also sell bits of the noose to the watching crowd – the noose used to hang someone was considered lucky. Another way the hangman might earn a few extra pennies would be to charge people to come up to the gallows and take some of the death sweat from the body. It was thought that rubbing this sweat on any patch of bad skin would heal it.

By the Law You are Dead

A hangman's task began at a trial when a criminal was sentenced to death.

THE HANGMAN would place his hand on the head of the condemned and call out *'dead, dead, dead, by the law you are dead'.* This is why the hangman was sometimes referred to as the Doomster.

On the day of an execution, Perth would be buzzing. An execution was like a big sporting event, people flocked to the city from far afield to watch. The city drummer marched up and down the streets beating the dead beat – at ten in the morning, again at eleven, and once more at noon. The condemned would be led from the Tolbooth to the cross of Perth, or placed on a cart with the hangman sitting alongside escorted by a guard up to the Burghmuir. If the body was to be left in chains once the hanging had taken place, the hangman would have to cut down the corpse and lay it on a table. There the bowels were removed and buried at the foot of the gallows, before the body, wrapped in chains, was placed back on the gibbet. It wasn't just a gruesome career, it was also a dangerous one. Sometimes in an effort to stop an execution, the hangman would be targeted by an angry mob.

At the end of his working day, the hangman, dirty and tired, would still have to take the horses back into town, often running the gauntlet through an angry crowd pelting him with rocks and stones. Meanwhile, the city magistrates would end the day of an execution by having a hearty meal at the taxpayers' expense in the council chambers.

Highland Robber Chief Hanged

In the reign of James I of Scotland, a highland chief plundered a widow's house.

THE CHIEF took everything of value, leaving her destitute. As he and his men prepared to leave, the poor widow angrily spat that she would never again wear shoes until she had personally reported the outrage to the king. The chief told her she was wrong, as she would indeed wear shoes long before she had seen the king. He ordered his men to grab the woman and hold her down, whilst he directed others to fetch horseshoes and nail them to the feet of the poor wretch. Somehow, the almost crippled woman made her way to Perth, where the king was holding court, and reported the crime. The king was incensed and ordered that the sheriff, from the county where the crime took place, arrest the perpetrator – adding that if the sheriff failed to do so, he would be executed instead.

The chief was arrested and taken to stand trial at Perth. He was found guilty and sentenced to hang. Before his execution, a shirt was made bearing the image of a highlander nailing a horseshoe onto a woman's foot. The chief was made to wear the shirt on the gallows.

Jacobites Poison the Hangman

George Penny tells a tale of two Jacobites who took part in the uprising of 1745-6 who were sentenced to hang in Perth.

ON THEIR WAY up to the place of execution, the hangman was suddenly seized with a violent illness. This happened shortly after he stopped for a drink. The supporters of the two Jacobite prisoners had poisoned him and the executioner was said to have died by the roadside in great agony.

The prisoners weren't off the hook though, as city officials offered another condemned man a pardon if he carried out the execution. He agreed and the two Jacobites were hanged. Penny also remarked that the man who had agreed to carry out the execution in return for his freedom was later himself hanged – it was decided that the magistrates had no legal right to offer him his freedom.

Penny provides no date for the event but it may be connected to an article in the September 1746 edition of the *Scots Magazine*, which ties in very nicely with Penny's account. The article describes how on 19 September 1746, a Captain Crosby, who had deserted from the British Army in Flanders and landed in Scotland with French Jacobite troops, was shot in Perth. Also executed that day, according to the article, were two other deserters who had left the government army to join Bonnie Prince Charlie. According to the article, the Perth hangman absconded, so the executioner from Stirling was called for but he died on the road. Perhaps he was indeed poisoned, there would have been time and opportunity to arrange it. With no hangman available, a prisoner from the Tolbooth was persuaded to do the deed.

* * *

Great Escape Against All the Odds

Bonnie Prince Charlie's exhausted and ragged army had been retreating for months and, despite a victory over the Government forces commanded by General Hawley at Falkirk on 17 January 1746, by February the Jacobite garrison in Perth had joined in the retreat north. Government troops closely followed the retreating Jacobites.

ONE GROUP of government soldiers turned up at Strathallan Castle about seventeen miles west of Perth. The 4th Viscount Strathallan was at the time away fighting with the Jacobite army; he would later die at the Battle of Culloden (16 April 1746). The soldiers were met by 85-year-old James Lawson who was in charge of the farm and keeper of the estate's woods. He could only stand by helplessly as the castle was looted. Lawson was seized and warned that he would be killed unless he told the officer-in-charge where the silver plate was hidden. The old man claimed the Strathallan family did not have any hidden plate. He was slung on a horse to accompany the troops as they made their way to Perth. Lawson was at the time suffering terribly from a hernia and in a lot of pain so he informed the officer of some plate buried near the castle. When it was dug up, the soldiers were not impressed as it was only pewter and not silver.

At the ford near Kinkell, the officer stopped his troop, ordered some of his men to place a noose around Lawson's neck, and to sling the other end of the rope over the branch of a tree. Lawson was told that if he did not disclose the whereabouts of the Strathallan silver, he would be hanged on the spot. By now, the old man was exhausted and he told his captors to do with him as they wished, as he was past caring. The officer ordered him cut down, stating he would be taken to Perth to hang in front of the Duke of Cumberland and General Hawley.

On the road to Perth, a younger officer tried to make the old man more comfortable. Once they reached Perth, Lawson was thrown into the Tolbooth. Things did not rest well for Lawson as he lay in his cell, for the next day he was to be tried by the Duke of Cumberland, son of George II, who, later, after his victory at the Battle of Culloden would more than earn his sobriquet of 'the Butcher', and General Hawley known then amongst his own troops as 'Hangman Hawley'.

The next morning, Lawson was taken in front of Cumberland and Hawley but the young officer who had shown the old man some kindness on the way to Perth argued passionately in the old man's defence. He persuaded the two military commanders that he thought Lawson was telling the truth about there being no silver plate hidden, because even when faced with death Lawson never changed his story. Cumberland and Hawley, probably to Lawson's amazement, threw the case out and he was freed. The young officer had the old man escorted to a lodging house at the outskirts of Perth and he personally paid for him to stay there until he had built up enough strength to head back to Strathallan Castle.*

According to Robert Scott Fittis, James Lawson worked at Strathallan Castle from 1727 until 1755 – quite a remarkable man who deserves to be remembered.

Killing in the Kirkgate

In 1720, a dance master, by the name of Mr Daroch, lived and taught dancing in the Kirk Gate.

ONE DAY, he decided that he would put on a party for his pupils. The evening started very successfully. Every one was having a great time until a group of drunken soldiers crashed the party and immediately the atmosphere changed. The soldiers were rowdy, rude, and spoiling for a fight. Daroch threw the soldiers out of his premises but the altercation spilled out on to the street.

One officer, a 28-year-old from Plymouth called Baver, squared up to Daroch. The officer was later to say *'and falling to beat him, then he turns to me, where he is stronger then* [sic] *I, he dirted me all upon the streets'*. Later, in the early hours of the morning, Baver went to wash at the public water pump in the street and found the dance master already there. Baver, who claimed he had another soldier as an accomplice, crept up on the unsuspecting dance master and hit him over the head with a stout stick. Daroch turned around and started grappling with Baver. It seems Daroch was then grabbed and had his arms held by the officer's accomplice while Baver ran him through with his sword. As Daroch lay dying on the street, the two soldiers fled.

* * *

Daroch's body was found soon afterwards. Several people remembered the fight between Daroch and the soldiers that occurred the night before. A large crowd made their way to Baver's lodging house where he was dragged out of his bed and frogmarched to the court, which was sitting at the time. After that trial had concluded, the court tried the army officer and he was found guilty. The hangman was called for and the soldier was hanged at the bottom of the High Street within six hours of the murder.

Robert Scott Fittis says in his *Antiquities of Perthshire* that as a result of the murder and the speed of the officer's execution, a new law was passed. It stipulated that south of the River Forth sentence of death could not be carried out before thirty days had passed, and before forty days north of the Forth.

The Irish Way to Die

George Penny in his "Traditions of Perth" tells of two Irishmen who were sentenced to hang in Perth.

THIS MUSt have been before 1750 as there is no record of the hanging in the *Encyclopaedia of Scottish Executions*, which covers the period 1750-1963. Penny's account tells of two Irishmen who were found guilty of committing highway robbery and sentenced to hang. The first man was dispatched without much trouble. The second decided he was going to go with a bit of style. He refused the services of a minister and instead decided to loudly sing a hymn, belting it out at the top of his voice – he then knelt to pray. His prayer was full of blasphemous remarks and at the end he thanked God that he was going to a better place free from rascally judges who would condemn a man for his place of birth. He stood up and loudly declared to the astonished crowd that he would show them all how an Irishman should die. He threw off his neck cloth, kicked off his shoes, put the noose over his head, and launched himself into oblivion before the stunned hangman had time to react. The crowd were very unsympathetic to the man, as they preferred a more conservative hanging but it is a great tale. If one was sentenced to be hanged, this surely would be the way to go, rebellious to the end!

Dog Solves Crime in Muthill

In 1750, Alexander McCowan lived in the village of Comrie with his wife and young son.

HE WAS ALSO seeing another woman who was a maid in Crieff. One day McCowan said to his wife:

'There is no work for me here, let's start a new life. We should move to Edinburgh, but do not tell your family or friends until we have settled there'.

His wife agreed and the family prepared to travel. Some weavers in the village of Muthill, south of Crieff, later saw them resting in what is now the park.

A week or two later, a dog walked into Muthill carrying something in its mouth. It was a human arm. The dog was chained up and was not fed for a few days. When the hungry dog was released, it went to the one place it knew it could get food, a shallow grave outside the village. In the grave were the remains of a woman and child, both had had their throats cut from ear

169

to ear. The villagers remembered McCowan resting with a woman and young boy and they were called for. They identified the bodies. McCowan was arrested in Edinburgh. He was sent to Perth to stand trial for murder and when he was found guilty, he was sentenced to hang.

McCowan was led up to the Burghmuir. Before he was hanged, his right hand, the hand that had held the murder weapon, was placed on a block of wood and the hangman chopped it off with an axe. His arm was nailed to the gallows. The noose was placed around McCowan's neck and he was pushed from the ladder but the rope snapped and McCowan hit the ground with a thud. He was overjoyed thinking that he had escaped justice but unfortunately for him a new length of rope was found and he was hanged a second time. That time everything went according to plan.

There is another story connected to the execution. It is said that after the body of McCowan had been cut down, the hangman cut the noose up and threw its lengths into the crowd so people could keep them for luck. One of the lengths of rope supposedly hit a heavily pregnant woman on the belly. She was reported to have given birth a few days later to a wee baby boy, who was missing his lower right arm. A nice story, perhaps an urban myth. Who knows?

That's My Boy

In June 1751, James Robertson, Hugh Knox, and Knox's son James were accused of horse stealing and highway robbery.

ROBERTSON and Hugh Knox were found guilty and sentenced to hang. James Knox being under eighteen years of age was sent to the plantations. Robertson and Knox were hanged on the 12th of July that year.

On 14 May 1753, Robert Davidson, George Bruce, and his 14-year-old son David were tried for robbery. The two older men were found guilty and executed on 22 June but the young boy broke down in court. He declared that his father had threatened to shoot him by holding a loaded pistol to his chest if he did not join in the crimes. The court showed young David mercy and he was freed.

* * *

A Jacobite Hero Hanged in Perth

John Dhu Cameron was a sergeant in the French army when he heard that Bonnie Prince Charlie had landed in Scotland in August 1745.

CAMERON was desperate to join the Jacobite army so headed for Scotland as soon as he could. He fought with his prince at the Battle of Culloden and following the Jacobite defeat he, like many others, became a fugitive, hiding in the hills and woods from the government troops who were mercilessly hunting down Jacobites.

Cameron gathered together a band of men and fought a guerrilla campaign using hit-and-run tactics to attack those who were supporters of the government. He became a sort of Robin Hood figure, as he would often leave food he had captured at the doors of persecuted Jacobites. During one raid, a man was unfortunately killed.

Cameron was high on the government's most wanted list. He was eventually captured when a farmer in Rannoch betrayed him to government soldiers while he was sleeping in the farmer's barn. Cameron was sent to Perth and tried for robbery and murder. He was found guilty and sentenced to hang. But when the hangman stepped forward to place his hand on Cameron's head and say the words '*dead, dead, dead, by the law you are dead*', Cameron resisted violently. The hangman thought better of things and beat a hasty retreat. John Dhu Cameron was executed on the Burghmuir on 23 November 1753. Afterwards his body was hung in chains.

Dr Archibald Cameron, brother of the chief of Clan Cameron and a surgeon during the '45, is said to have been the last Jacobite to die for the cause. He was hanged at Tyburn in London on 7 June 1753 but as John Dhu Cameron was executed in November 1753 it could be argued that he was the last Jacobite to pay the ultimate price for supporting Bonnie Prince Charlie.

Murder on the Road

William Doig was a travelling chapman who sold wares door-to-door around the villages and towns of Perthshire.

HE MET fellow chapman, 14-year-old Patrick Maxton, on the road near the village of Muthill. Maxton, who was a few years older than Patrick, set about the young lad, beat him to death, before stealing the dead boy's pack.

When he was caught and tried, he seemed to be very remorseful for the wicked life he had led, apologising publicly for swearing, Sabbath breaking, and letting down his parents. Strangely, the one thing that he did not feel that sorry for is killing young Patrick Maxton. For the crime, his sentence was to be fed on bread and water until his execution. He was hanged in Perth on 13 June 1755. After his execution, his body was handed over to a local surgeon to be dissected.

Killed For an Ounce of Tea

When Anne Adams persuaded a Perth shopkeeper to give her an ounce of tea on tick, she probably never imagined such a trifling act would lead to her brutal slaying.

WHEN her husband, 36-year-old weaver Donald McCraw, walked into the shop and was asked for payment for the tea, he went home in a terrible rage and killed his wife, despite her being eight months pregnant.

According to McCraw, he was told by a neighbour to run for his life and he did indeed flee. His conscience however got the better of him and he handed himself into the authorities.

Broadsides were popular pamphlets full of titillating news, the last words of criminals condemned to die, and ballads, which were sold by chapmen. The life story of McCraw was published after his execution in a Broadside titled *The Last Confession and Dying Words of Donald McCraw*. In the article, McCraw told of being born in Inverness-shire to honest industrious people and how he learned the trade of weaving and moved to Glasgow for work before relocating to Perth. He told of having a violent temper and his wife an unhappy life, he also admitted to frequently beating her. McCraw recounted how much he regretted his life and the killing of his wife and unborn child. Donald McCraw was hanged in Perth on 13 November 1795.

Terror in the Tollhouse

William McRitchie, the toll-keeper of the Edinburgh Road Tollhouse, was waiting up late on the night of 12 November 1816 for some people returning from a party at Pitcaithly House.

AT MIDNIGHT, there was a loud bang on the door and a man outside demanded some beer. When McRitchie replied that he had none, the person asked for water. McRitchie told him that plenty water could be got from the roadside. Then there was another request, this time for whisky but with an offer to pay a shilling for it. Again, the toll-keeper refused. By now McRitchie had realised that there were several men outside. He told them to go on to Perth but they replied they had come from Haddington, were very weary, and could not go into town without first getting something to drink. One man then rapped on the window with a shilling but when McRitchie drew closer to the window, he noticed the man was carrying a pistol. The man threatened to blow the toll-keeper's brains out unless he let them in. McRitchie could see there were three men: two wearing red jackets, the other a great coat. He let the men into the Tollhouse, whereupon they made a demand for money, which came with threats to kill McRitchie's wife Emilia and harm the couple's children.

While Emilia handed the robbers the couple's personal money, William McRitchie took out the day's takings from a drawer. There were two forged guinea notes, which were worthless, and a real guinea note. He handed them over to the men. Meanwhile, in a back room and unknown to the robbers, the McRitchies' servant had opened a window and had made her escape. Although one of the criminals chased her for a short distance, the young woman escaped and went to seek assistance. When she returned with help, the assailants had fled leaving the traumatised toll-keeper and his family very shaken.

A few days later, Lydia Barber tried to pay for goods with a forged note. Mr Christie, the shopkeeper, informed the authorities. Lydia was married to James Mitchell and when his house was searched, a loaded pistol and the other forged note were discovered. Hiding in a coal cellar at the house was a man named John Larg who was also arrested. Mitchell and Larg were tried for the crime of stouthrief, the violent robbery of a house. The third man involved was identified as Alexander Steel but he managed to escape justice. Mitchell and Larg were found guilty and hanged in Perth on 28 February 1817.

* * *

Pillar of the Community Turned Wife Killer

*John Chisholm was a respected churchgoing merchant who ran a
shop in South Street for some forty years.*

AT ONE TIME, the 76-year-old had also been a special constable in the city.
For all he gave the impression of being a respectable and pleasant man to
the outside world, he was in fact a brutal and violent husband behind
closed doors. His first wife had warned him that one day he would hang for
his violent behaviour. Her prophecy came true when Chisholm beat his
second wife to death and was indeed sentenced to meet his end on the gallows.

The strain put on prisoners awaiting execution is evidenced by the
physical and mental state of Janet Stewart who was sentenced to hang at
the same time as Chisholm. Stewart had murdered her brother-in-law but
was granted a temporary stay of execution due to the deterioration of her
physical appearance and mental exhaustion. During that stay, evidence
that questioned her conviction surfaced.

While Stewart was informed of the postponement, Chisholm's
execution was set to go ahead. He was held in the condemned cell but as his
date with death drew closer, the elderly man was moved to the prison's sick
ward. Chisholm was in good spirits and seemed to have come to terms with
his approaching death. On the day of the execution, Reverend Kennedy of
the West Church spent most of the morning in prayer with the prisoner.
Chisholm's nerve gave way a little when they came to restrain him. He was
led out to the scaffold and after drinking a glass of wine that was handed to
him led the singing of Psalm 130, for when he was asked if he had any last
words, Chisholm requested the singing of a hymn and the wish was
granted. The old man belted out the hymn at the top of his voice. When the
hangman had made his last adjustments, the lever was pulled and
Chisholm went to face his God without a struggle.

The Last Public Show

*The last public hanging in Perth was that carried out on
Joseph Bell in 1866. **

BELL HAD LAIN in wait hidden in the undergrowth one December
evening in 1865 on the road between Blairingone and Vicar's Bridge in
Kinross-shire. He waited patiently, his hands caressing the shotgun he

was carrying until the bread delivery cart of William Muirhead & Sons driven by John Miller passed. (There is some disagreement as to the driver's name. Geoff Holder in his *Perthshire Murders* names him as John Miller whereas both the *Alloa Advertiser* of 26 May 1866 and the *Dundee Courier* of 23 May 1866 name him as Alexander M'Ewan. The *Perthshire Advertiser* of 24 May 1866 on the other hand names the dead man as Alexander M'Queen.)

Miller's bread delivery route took him to Dollar, Muckart, Vicar's Bridge, Blairingone, Forestmill, and Clackmannan before returning to the depot at Alloa. He would be paid for his bread in cash and usually carried a fair amount of money.

When the cart passed Bell's hiding place, the would-be robber stepped out from the shadows and fired at the driver, blowing half his face away and fatally wounding him. After robbing the dying man, Bell made his escape. But, as a well known ne'er-do-well, he was soon in the frame for this violent crime: someone matching his description was spotted in the vicinity of the murder carrying a gun. Bell was arrested at a friend's home in Tillicoultry on 20 December, a day after the crime had been committed. When he was apprehended, Bell had money on his person that matched the amount and description that the driver of the bread cart was carrying – the amount and denomination of the money having been documented in a pocket book found on the victim. Bell's footprints were found near the crime scene and sometime before the robbery and murder he had asked Robert Wright, a weaver, if he would help him rob a bread van (asking Wright to hold the horse while he took care of the driver). Wright had replied that he was not that kind of man and Bell had responded by saying he was only joking.

Bell was tried for murder in Perth, 24-25 April 1866, and found guilty. For his crime, he was sentenced to hang. He was locked up in the condemned cell of Perthshire County Prison, which stood behind the courthouse in Tay Street (today a car park). The time and date of the execution was set for 8-10am, 22 May 1866.

After complaining about his diet of bread and water in a letter to the sheriff, claiming that he was used to good living, Bell's diet was changed to food that was better than the rest of his fellow inmates. Bell spent the days before his execution writing letters and poetry in the company of two spiritual advisers – the prison chaplain, the Reverend Mr St Clair of

St Stephen's Church, and the Reverend Robert Milne of the West Church -with whom he discussed religious matters.

Despite 105 witness statements against him and the evidence of the trial, Bell continued to protest his innocence of the crime. He claimed the evidence of his guilt was circumstantial, the jury were misled by press articles against him, that he was being made an example of due to the large number of recent violent crimes in the area, and that as he was an Englishman, he was being discriminated against. No matter how hard the two churchmen tried to get Bell to confess, he steadfastly refused stating that he was as innocent as a newly-born child.

Bell was treated as a celebrity while in prison. He was allowed several visits: from his parents, brother, sister, and a male cousin. His aged father was visibly shaken when he saw his son. The old man sat rocking on a chair uttering the words '*Oh my Joseph, my poor Joseph*', until he noticed some scripture on the wall of the meeting room above his son's cell. When Bell Senior saw the religious writing, he cheered up and equated it to the fate of his son. Bell was also visited by an aunt and uncle and despite being advised by his uncle to confess, still declared himself to be innocent.

It is worth noting the *Perthshire Advertiser* of 24 May 1866 stated:

'If Bell did not commit the murder for which he was condemned, his firmness and calm resolution stamps him as a heroic man'.

The paper however argued that all the evidence of the trial pointed to Bell in fact being guilty. The *Alloa Advertiser* of 22 May 1866 also made comment on Bell's claims of innocence:

'His declarations of innocence were all more or less made in that stereotyped form of gibbet literature that has come down from time immoral, and were merely strongly worded assertions, without being backed by anything like the shadow of a shade of proof in their support'.

The general public certainly thought Bell was guilty. A petition asking for a reprieve was not signed by one person and Bell's attempt to obtain a reprieve ended in failure. Bell, who signed some of his 'cell poetry' the Dying Joseph Bell, was going to have to pay the ultimate price for his crime.

Whilst incarcerated, Bell was persuaded by some friends to have his

picture taken. Commercial photographer John Henderson was comm-
issioned for the task. Bell, along with Lord Provost (Sheriff) Barclay, and the
city magistrates, posed for a photograph. Bell was photographed sitting
looking at a watch he had borrowed from one of the wardens. Sheriff
Barclay urged Bell to pose for two other photographs: one standing and
another sitting at a table examining an open Bible. The sheriff had twenty
pictures printed for Bell who distributed them among his family and friends
as well as the wardens, the sheriff, and officials.

As the day of the execution drew nearer, it became apparent that the
town gallows, which had to be brought out of storage, had parts missing
and were in a dilapidated state. It was decided to borrow Aberdeen's gallows.
They had last been used when John Kellocher was hanged in Perth in 1849
for killing his landlady at Buttergask (by Blackford).

The gallows arrived from Aberdeen on Saturday the 19th. At 2am on
Monday 21 May, those who lived in the vicinity of the County Prison were
awoken by the sound of the workmen erecting the scaffolding and gallows
-they were finished by 11am. Crowds of curious onlookers milled around
the gallows, which were built at the southern end of the prison, in front of
Greyfriars Burial Ground. The scaffold stood some fifteen feet tall and was
surrounded by a fence six feet in height, erected with sufficient room
between the scaffold and fence to accommodate the special constables and
police officers who would be on duty during the execution. The scaffold was
draped in black cloth, which must have given the morbid construction an
even more sinister look. As the crowds gathered, lay preachers read
passages of the Bible and condemned anyone who might be planning to
come and watch the execution. A young boy who had obtained one of Bell's
photographs let those, who no doubt paid a few pence, have a look at what
he claimed to be 'a true and correct likeness of Joseph Bell'.

At 7pm on Sunday 20 May, the train from London pulled into Perth
Station. One of the passengers who stepped from one of the first class
carriages was met by another man and hurriedly shown to a waiting
carriage. The man was William Calcraft, the hangman. He had been met
by a plain-clothed policeman and together they made their way to the
County Prison. The hangman was accommodated at the prison until the
execution, having his meals brought to him, supplied by the *Salutation*

Hotel. The hangman had arrived a day earlier than the public expected so as to miss the large crowds the authorities anticipated would gather to see his arrival.

On the day of the execution, 22 May, at 7:30am, Calcraft made his way to the condemned cell and pinioned the arms and legs of the condemned man. Bell was taken upstairs to the schoolroom where Sheriff Barclay, the Lord Provost, the magistrates of Perth, and the city's High Constables, were waiting. Bell, who at the time of his arrest was very fit and strong, and boasted he could lift and move a half-ton weight a distance of sixty yards, could walk at a rate of five and a half miles an hour, and run a mile in four and a half minutes, now looked haggard and emaciated. His shrunken eyes were red with dark rings around them and he stooped forward as he walked. The stress and strain of the last few months had clearly taken a toll.

After the minister read a passage from the Bible, the Lord Provost addressed Bell. The provost offered to listen to any last statements and to try and meet any last requests. Bell thanked those who had looked after him while he was incarcerated and again stated that he was innocent of the crime. He was given a glass of wine, which he devoured. The party formed a processional order: the Town Sergeant followed by the Lord Provost, the magistrates, Sheriff Barclay, two prison wardens, Bell, and the Reverends St Clair and Milne walked either side of the prisoner; the police superintendent and the governor of the prison were followed by the High Constables. As they left the schoolroom, the party was met by the hangman. Together, they made their way along a long corridor, through a door, and climbed the steps of the scaffold. Bell was positioned under the beam. Calcraft placed a white hood over Bell's head followed by a noose which he fastened. As Calcraft went about the business of fastening the rope, Bell stood swaying slightly from side to side. The only noise heard was that made by a few women in the crowd weeping. Calcraft shook the condemned man by the hand. Bell was heard to whisper:

'*I die an innocent man*'.

He then added in a louder tone:

'*Good Bye, I'm quite ready*'.

At that, the bolt was drawn and, at seven minutes past eight on the morning of 22 May 1866, the last man to be publicly executed in Perth dropped to his death.

The crowd at the hanging was well below the number expected. Only around 3,000 people, mainly young girls and boys, were present. Many of those who worked in Perth had been warned by their employers that if they did not show up for work on time on the day of the execution, without a good excuse to explain their lateness, they would be sacked. This and the fact that in 1866 people no longer regarded watching someone being hanged as entertainment kept down the numbers.

There was a backlash over the way Bell had been treated in the County Prison. An article published in the *Perthshire Advertiser* on 31 May 1866 claimed that Bell was given so much freedom in prison that he tried to hang himself with a piece of rope. The article's author pondered how a man condemned to hang could obtain a length of rope. He also stated that on the day before his execution, Bell gave the authorities a clasp knife he had been hiding. (Again questions as to how he had this knife in his possession were asked.) The article further states that people were angered at the amount of leniency and '*petting*' that Bell, a man who '*waited behind a hedge till his victim came up, and then deliberately shot him*', received whilst in prison. In particular, the clergy who it was claimed utterly spoiled Bell in a useless attempt to reform him, were lambasted. Quoting the *Dundee Advertiser*, the article elaborated on the petting and pampering of murderers:

'*What does a father of a family do with a guilty or rebellious child? Does he not seclude him from the rest of the family. Does he not cut him off, for the time being, from the privileges of the obedient members, in food and liberty, and the light of their father's favour, until the little rebel comes to himself, and is restored? What would be thought of a father pampering or coaxing a stubborn little fellow to do the right thing, and the more the child resisted the more to pet him? What would be thought if he made him an object of such interest that a photographer would be engaged to take the likeness of the little prisoner in the garret or nursery in order to distribute it among his brothers and sisters that they might learn a lesson from his example?*'

It is easy to see how the authorities and clergy came in for a great deal of criticism for the way they treated a man who committed such a violent, vicious, and cowardly crime on an unarmed man going about his daily business. The driver of the bread cart never knew what hit him, when taken to a nearby farm the poor man was not even aware that he had been shot despite missing half his face. Bits of his jaw bone were found lying on the road and his eye had been blown out. He thought he had simply fallen from his cart. Joseph Bell had given him no warning or chance to hand over the money before firing the fatal shot.

After giving a talk a few years ago in the Duchally Hotel (near Auchterarder), an old man approached the author and told him that his grandfather had walked from Falkland in Fife to witness the last hanging in Perth.

No Longer a Public Event

Forty-five-year-old George Chamers was found guilty of robbing and killing John Millar, the 64-year-old keeper of the Tollhouse on Blackhill, near the village of Braco, on 21 December 1869.

MILLAR was found lying with a smashed skull amidst his ransacked house. His supper of boiled ham, cheese, and bread lay on a table uneaten. Money, a silver watch, and clothing were missing. Chamers was a vagrant who wandered the countryside taking occasional labouring jobs or sang in the streets for a few pennies. He had only just been released, the day before the murder, from Alloa jail, where he had been held for being drunk and disorderly. He was arrested and found guilty for the murder of Millar, although he denied any involvement to the very end.

Chamers' execution was the first in Scotland that was not carried out publicly but rather privately, within the walls of Perth General Prison. At his trial, Chamers listened to most of the evidence with an air of distain but he nonetheless broke down and cried when the death sentence was read out – his sobs almost drowning out the Lord Justice-Clerk. An effort was made to have the sentence overturned, as much of the evidence seemed to be circumstantial but the Home Secretary who, after conferring with the judge, saw no reason to do so, denied this. When this news reached Chamers that the death sentence would stand, he again broke down. In the condemned cell, he passed the time reading the Bible. At night, he seemed to sleep well, despite being handcuffed and watched over by a warden sitting in his cell.

In the days before his execution, Chamers was allowed a visit from his two brothers and his brother-in-law. Chamers' brothers had come down from the North-East and his brother-in-law from Arbroath. The day before the execution, the prison chaplain and a local minister visited Chamers and the day was spent in prayer. That night, he understandably slept very little, using the time to talk to the chaplain who spent the night with him. Breakfast was tea and bread. Chamers was said to have drunk the tea but did not eat anything. The chaplain spent some time trying to persuade Chamers to confess to the killing but he continued to protest that he was innocent.

At seven-thirty in the morning, the magistrates and officials arrived. They were led out into the courtyard in front of the governor's house where the scaffold stood. The hangman, William Calcraft, who had arrived the night before on the mail train from the south, was in the condemned cell preparing the prisoner. Chamers was composed and calm and even helped the hangman with the restraining straps. Just after the bells of St John's had struck eight o'clock, the condemned man was led out, accompanied by the executioner and the minister. The prisoner walked unaided and seemed to be in a hurry, walking at a quick pace. He even ran up the steps to the scaffold, leaving his escort behind, struggling to catch up. As the rope was placed around his neck and a white hood was pulled over his head, Chamers was heard to protest his innocence once more. The minister asked if he had any last words. Chamers simply bid everyone a last farewell. His last declaration of innocence had just left his lips when the trapdoor sprung open and he fell to his death. At that point a black flag was raised over the prison informing a small crowd outside the walls that George Chamers was dead.

The End

Stanislaw Myszka, a former soldier in the Polish Army, was sentenced to hang in Perth for the brutal murder in 1947 of Catherine McIntyre at Tower Cottage, near Kenmore.

THE HANGING of Myszka was the first execution in Perth since Alexander Edmonstone was hanged for robbery and murder in 1909.

During a violent robbery, Myszka had tied Catherine McIntyre up in her home and, as she lay defenceless, beat her to death with the butt of his shotgun. At his trial in Perth on 6 January 1948 Stanislaw pled not guilty by reason of temporary insanity. After hearing all the evidence, it took the jury just twenty minutes to return with a unanimous guilty verdict.

Myszka was sentenced to be executed. This was carried out on 6 February 1948 at Perth Prison. It is interesting to note that although reports of the execution were printed on the front page of many newspapers, the story was not sensationalised as in previous executions. While the crime and trial were recorded in detail, the hanging was reported in quite a sober manner. The *Dundee Evening Telegraph* printed on the day of the execution gives the story but one column on its front page.

The Polish national was hanged at eight in the morning within the walls of the prison. A small crowd gathered outside the gates, amongst them four women. The prisoner went to his death in a calm manner. According to some newspaper reports, Myszka did not utter any last words before the executioner Albert Pierrepoint hanged him. After the execution, a notice stating it had been carried out in accordance with the law was pinned to the gate. The death of Stanislaw Myszka signalled the end of a dark era in the history of Perth.

The last person hanged in Scotland was Henry John Burnett, who was hanged for murder in Aberdeen in 1963.

* * *

Bibliography

PRIMARY SOURCES

Perth Burgh Sentences, Death Warrants, and Associated Papers
B59/26/11/1-3, 1696-1834. 'Papers relating to crimes, prisoners, sentences and punishments, with details of crimes, defendants, victims and witnesses, not only in Perthshire but also in Forfarshire, Stirlingshire and other places in Scotland.' Perth & Kinross Council Archive.

City and Royal Burgh of Perth Miscellaneous/Legal Papers including Perth Sheriff Court Papers
PE 48-58, 1540-1983. Perth & Kinross Council Archive.

SECONDARY SOURCES

BOOKS

Adams, Norman – *Scottish Bodysnatchers* (Musselburgh: Goblinshead, 2002)

Antoniewicz, Roben and **Paul S. Philippou** – *The Early Photographers of Perthshire* (Perth: Tippermuir Books Ltd, 2016)

Baxter, Peter – *Perth: past & present, Volume I* (Perth: John McKinlay, 1928)

Buchanan, Lachlan D. – *Stories From Perth's History* (Perth: Melvin Press, 1978)

Cant, James – *Memorabilia of the City of Perth* (Perth: William Morison, 1806)

Cowan, Samuel – *The Ancient Capital of Scotland ,Volume I and II* (London: Simpkin, Marshall, Hamilton, Kent & Company, 1904)

Farquhar, Reverend T. S. – *The Episcopal History of Perth 1689-1894* (Perth: J. H. Jackson, 1894)

Fittis, Robert Scott – *Witches and Warlocks of Perthshire* (Edinburgh: 1878)

Fittis, Robert Scott – *Ecclesiastical Annals of Perth* (Edinburgh: J. Gemmell, 1885)

Fittis, Robert Scott – *The Weaver's Records* (Edinburgh: 1888)

Holder, Geoff – *Perthshire Murders* (Stroud: Amberley Publishing, 2010)

Horan, Martin – *Chambers Scottish Executions, Assassinations and Murders* (Edinburgh: Chambers, 1990)

Jillings, Karen – *Scotland's Black Death: the foul death of the English* (Stroud: Tempus, 2003)

Lawson, John Parker – *The Book of Perth* (Edinburgh: Thomas G. Stevenson, 1847)

Marshall, Thomas Hay – *History of Perth: from the earliest period to the present time* (Perth: J. Fisher, 1849)

Peacock, David – *Perth: its Annals and its Archives* (Perth: Thomas Richardson, 1849)

Penny, George – *Traditions of Perth* (Perth: Dewar, Sidey, Morison, Peat & Drummond, 1836)

Sievwright, William – *Historical Sketch of the General Prison For Scotland at Perth* (Perth: Alexander Wright, 1894)

Sievwright, William – *Historical sketch of the old depot; or, Prison for French prisoners-of-war at Perth* (Perth: Alexander Wright, 1894)

Stavert, Marion L. – *Perth a Short History* (Perth: Perth & Kinross District Libraries, 1991)

Strachan, David, *Perth: a Place in History* ʼ (Perth: Perth & Kinross Heritage Trust, 2011)

Warner, Gerald – *Tales of the Scottish Highlands* (London: Shepheard-Walwyn, 1987)

Young, Alex F. – *The Encyclopaedia of Scottish Executions 1750-1963* (Kent: Eric Dobby Publishing Ltd, 1998)

BROADSIDES

The Last Confession and Dying Words of Donald McCraw – APS 4.83.19, 6.365 (098)

Broadside Regarding the Murder of Mr Daroch the Dance Master - RY IIIc 36 (070)

JOURNALS

Scotia American – Canadian Journal of Scottish Studies, Volume XI, 1987

The Perth Saturday Journal, 28 August 1841

MAGAZINES

The Scots Magazine, September 1746, June 1755, November 1756, June 1762, December 1772, May 1812

NEWSPAPERS

Aberdeen Evening Express, 9 November 1891

Aberdeen Journal, 4 November 1893

Aberdeen Press & Journal, 11 October 1876, 20 September 1899

Alloa Advertiser, 26 May 1866

Arbroath Herald & Advertiser, 9 November 1923

Belfast Morning News, 18 December 1867

Birmingham Daily Post, 24 December 1862

Caledonian Mercury, 25 May 1730, 12 January 1755, 12 May 1755,
    8 September 1764, 16 May 1793, 1 July 1865, 19 September 1866

Derby Mercury, 27 September 1754, 31 January 1755

Derby Telegraph, 9 November 1891

Dublin Evening Mail, 6 November 1863

Dundee Advertiser, 28 November 1861, 25 May 1866, 21 September 1866,
    15 January 1889, 16 May 1890

Dundee Courier, 31 December 1844, 1 July 1845, 2 September 1845,
    7 February 1849, 23 May 1866, 29 October 1866, 9 October 1869,
    5 October 1870, 4 March 1873, 30 July 1874, 20 July 1875,
    18 June 1877, 6 May 1878, 2 January 1879, 16 December 1881,
    9 January 1882, 31 July 1883, 15 January 1884, 22 September 1885,
    5 April 1887, 14 November 1887, 27 June 1888, 24 July 1888,
    28 November 1888, 24 October 1889, 4 January 1895,
    9 October, 1895, 12 August 1896, 21 May 1897, 24 May 1897,
    30 September 1897, 23 August 1898, 14 September 1898,
    9 August, 1899, 20 September 1899, 6 November 1899, 11 April 1900,
    15 May 1900, 6 August 1901, 20 December 1902, 3 August 1903,
    6 July 1903, 28 December 1903, 17 March 1904, 1 April 1904,
    26 August 1904, 22 May 1905, 27 June 1905, 5 June 1910,
    16 December 1912, 1 January 1913, 28 April 1913, 29 April 1913,
    17 April 1914, 28 June 1917, 29 December 1919, 5 November 1923, 30
    April 1924, 8 August 1925, 11 August 1925, 31 March 1928,
    25 September 1928, 27 November 1928, 8 August 1933,
    15 August 1933, 19 August 1935, 21 August 1935, 2 December 1935,
    4 December 1937

Dundee Evening Post, 20 June 1902, 30 January 1903, 18 February 1903,
    11 March 1903, 23 October 1903, 16 May 1905

Dundee Evening Telegraph, 15 April 1879, 8 June 1882, 22 September 1885,
16 June 1888, 15 September 1897, 3 November 1899, 16 February 1903,
14 August 1903, 25 August 1904, 26 June 1905, 23 May 1907,
12 April 1910, 14 September 1916, 29 April 1924, 26 September 1924,
16 October 1924, 5 February 1925, 26 November 1928,
28 March 1929, 23 July 1929, 14 October 1937, 30 July 1938,
6 February 1948

Dundee People's Journal, 5 July 1884

Edinburgh Evening News, 7 October 1876

Fife Free Press & Kirkcaldy Guardian, 24 August 1935

Glasgow Herald, 7 May 1864, 15 May 1874

Inverness Courier, 4 October 1826, 7 November 1832

Lancashire Evening Post, 24 August 1935

Leeds Mercury, 4 May 1880

Morning Advertiser, 16 May 1837
  Montrose, Arbroath & Brechin Review, 3 July 1868

Northern Wig, 30 August 1935

Public Ledger & Daily Advertiser, 1 May 1812.

Perthshire Advertiser, 28 September 1865, 24 May 1866, 31 May 1866,
18 April 1870, 6 May 1942

Perthshire Courier, 23 January 1817, 21 September 1826, 12 October 1854

The Scotsman, 10 May 1837, 21 June 1927

Western Morning News, 15 October 1937

WEBSITES
https://canmore.org.uk

THE PUBLISHER

Tippermuir Books Ltd (*est.* 2009) is an independent publishing company based in Perth, Scotland.

OTHER TITLES FROM TIPPERMUIR BOOKS

Spanish Thermopylae (Paul S. Philippou, 2009)

Battleground Perthshire
(Paul S. Philippou & Robert A. Hands, 2009)

Perth: Street by Street
(Paul S. Philippou & Roben Antoniewicz, 2012)

Born in Perthshire
(Paul S. Philippou & Robert A. Hands, 2012)

In Spain with Orwell (Christopher Hall, 2013)

Trust (Ajay Close, 2014)

Perth: As Others Saw Us (Donald Paton, 2014)

Love All (Dorothy L. Sayers, 2015)

A Chocolate Soldier (David W. Millar, 2016)

The Early Photographers of Perthshire
(Roben Antoniewicz & Paul S. Philippou, 2016)

Taking Detective Novels Seriously:
The Collected Crime Reviews of Dorothy L. Sayers
(Dorothy L. Sayers and Martin Edwards, 2017)

Walking with Ghosts (Alan J. Laing, 2017)

FORTHCOMING

The Fair Maid of Perth: the Perth Edition
(Walter Scott, 2017)

The Tale o the Wee Mowdie
(Werner Holzwarth and Wolf Erlbruch,
translated by Matthew Mackie, 2017)

Wee Stories from the Crescent:
A Reminiscence of Perth's Hunter Crescent
(Anthony Camilleri, 2017)

All titles are available from
bookshops and online booksellers.

They can also be purchased directly at
www.tippermuirbooks.co.uk

Tippermuir Books Ltd can be contacted at
mail@tippermuirbooks.co.uk

TIPPERMUIR
· BOOKS LIMITED ·